10 HABITS FOR EFFECTIVE MINISTRY

Lowell O. Erdahl

10 HABITS
FOR EFFECTIVE
MINISTRY

◆

A Guide for
Life-Giving Pastors

Augsburg
MINNEAPOLIS

10 HABITS FOR EFFECTIVE MINISTRY
A Guide for Life-Giving Pastors

Scripture quotations, unless otherwise noted, are from the New Revised Standard Version Bible, copyright © 1989 by the division of Christian Education of the National Council of the Churches of Christ in the U.S.A. and used by permission.

Scripture quotations noted RSV are from the Revised Standard Version Bible, copyright © 1946, 1952, 1971 by the Division of Christian Education of the National Council of the Churches of Christ in the U.S.A. Used by permission.

Scripture quotations noted CEV are from the Contemporary English Version text, copyright © 1991, 1992 American Bible Society. Used by permission.

Scripture quotations noted NEB are from the New English Bible, copyright © 1961, 1970 by the Delegates of the Oxford University Press and the Syndics of the Cambridge University Press. Used by permission.

Cover design by David Meyer
Text design by James Satter

Library of Congress Cataloging-in-Publication Data

Erdahl, Lowell O.
    10 habits for effective ministry : a guide for life-giving pastors /
Lowell O. Erdahl.
        p.   cm.
    Includes bibliographical references.
    ISBN 0-8066-2990-8 (alk. paper)
    1. Clergy—Office.   2. Erdahl, Lowell O.   I. Title.   II. Title:
Ten habits for effective ministry
BV660.2.E73 1996
253'.2—dc20   96-20562
                                                                     CIP

The paper used in this publication meets the minimum requirements of American National Standard for Information Sciences—Permanence of Paper for Printed Library Materials, ANSI Z329.48-1984.   ∞

Manufactured in the U.S.A.   AF 9-2990

00   99   98   2   3   4   5   6   7   8   9   10

To Carol

Friend, Companion, Wife

Contents

Introduction

A great commission for pastors is concisely stated in Acts 5:20—"Go stand in the temple and speak to the people all the words of this Life." In the Revised Standard Version (RSV), the word "Life" is printed with a capital L. It witnesses to this purpose of Christ: "I came that they may have life, and have it abundantly" (John 10:10). Ten chapters later, John reports another even briefer great commission from Jesus: "As the Father has sent me, so I send you" (John 20:21). We are the recipients of Jesus' life-giving ministry. We are called and sent by Jesus to be life-giving pastors.

Nearly 150 years ago, the British preacher F. W. Robertson said in a sermon on the "The Illusiveness of Life":

> Remember, we are here to live and to die; in a few years it will all be over; meanwhile, what we have to do is to try to understand, and to help one another to understand, what it all means—what this strange and contradictory thing, which we call life, contains within it. [1]

This is essential to our business as pastors. We thank God for the understanding of life revealed in Jesus. But as Christian pastors, we are not only teachers conveying understanding. In Christ we have been given new life to live and new life to give. We are called in Christ to be life-giving pastors—proclaiming, bearing, and sharing in attitude, word, and action the new, abundant, full "Life," with a capital L, that Christ came to give.

Being entrusted with such a high calling moves us to awe and gratitude. It gives us a reason to get out of bed in the morning! But at the same time it also reminds us of our limitations and failures. If we have any self-awareness, we know that our ministries are not always life-giving. That has been true for me and I have seen it in others, especially during my dozen years as a bishop.

Some clergy have told me that they have no influence and that their ministries seem to have little effect in the lives of their congregations. This may sometimes be true, but from my perspective pastors have immense influence. The way we conduct our ministries is among the most significant factors shaping our parishes, and if we are honest we are compelled to confess that this influence is not always constructive. Although we are called to be life-giving ambassadors for a life-giving Christ, our ministries may fail to be life-enabling and may even be life-degrading. Although a teacher probably has more influence in the classroom than does a pastor in a parish, there are enough parallels to enable us to identify with educator Haim Ginott:

> I've come to the frightening conclusion that I am the decisive element in the classroom. It's my personal approach that creates the climate. It's my daily mood that makes the weather. As a teacher, I possess a tremendous power to make a child's life miserable or joyous. I can be a tool of torture or an instrument of inspiration. I can humiliate or humor, hurt or heal. In all situations it is my response that decides whether a crisis will be escalated or de-escalated and a child humanized or dehumanized.[2]

Reflection on effective, life-giving ministries prompts significant questions: What are the characteristics of life-giving pastors? How do their lives and ministries differ from those who are ineffective or life-destructive? What can be done to encourage and strengthen those qualities that enable and create life-giving ministry?

It is now nearly forty years since my ordination, and I hope that I have learned some things that can help answer those questions. It has been a long and sometimes faltering journey—ten years as solo pastor in a town church, five years on a seminary faculty, ten years as senior pastor of a large urban parish, and then a dozen years as a bishop. At this point in my pilgrimage I believe there are at least ten characteristics of pastors, ten qualities, ten modes of pastoral attitude and practice, that enable and enhance life-giving ministry. With the same broad meaning as in Robert Bellah's *Habits of the Heart*, and Stephen Covey's *Seven Habits of Highly-Effective People*, I have chosen to call them *Ten Habits for Effective Ministry.*

These ten are habits of heart, mind, and behavior. As life-giving pastors, our goal is not just to analyze and describe but to encourage, evoke, and enable the enhancement of these qualities in our lives. Some of these characteristics are like the "fruit of the Spirit" in Galatians 5:22. They come not from our striving but instead from our surrender and openness to the healing, life-transforming, life-giving Spirit of God. They are gifts, but they are tasks as well. Love, for example, is the first fruit of the Spirit, but it is also commanded by Jesus: "I give you a new commandment, that you love one another. Just as I love you, you also should love one another" (John 13:34). Developing the habits of life-giving ministry relates not only to our self-surrender but also to our self-awareness, and especially to our listening and our learning.

With Archippus we are called to "fulfill the ministry which you have received in the Lord" (Colossians 4:17, RSV). That happens when we, by the grace of God, are bearers of the life Christ came to give which is life "in all its fullness" (John 10:10 NEB). I hope that the reader will find my autobiographical reflections, shared learnings, and encouragements to be personally and pastorally helpful. If something in these pages helps to encourage, evoke and enable such effective, life-giving ministry, I will be grateful.

IN APPRECIATION

As I review what I have written, I must confess that it turned out to contain more autobiographical content than I had intended to include. When I raised concerns in this regard with my editor and others who read the manuscript, everyone encouraged me to "leave it in," and I have yielded to their advice. The personal dimensions of what I have shared remind me that in a sense I have been preparing to write this book all my life, and I am thankful for many more people than can be named in this note of appreciation.

Writing of effective ministry prompts me to express gratitude for the pastors who have helped shape my life, beginning with H. O. Mosby, who baptized and confirmed me, and Emil Ede, who was my intern supervisor. The congregations of Farmington Lutheran Church in Farmington, Minnesota, and University Lutheran Church of Hope in Minneapolis, and the coworkers with whom I served for a decade in each parish are remembered with thankfulness.

More specifically, I wish to personally thank all of those whom I invited to read and comment on the manuscript during the final stages of its development. All are clergy with diverse parish, teaching, and institutional church experience. Their comments concurred on many matters but were significantly different on others. I have tried to learn from them all. I know this book is better than it would have been without the gift of their insights and suggestions. With gratitude I list their names in alphabetical order: Myrwood Bagne, Marilyn Breckenridge, John Davis, Jan Erickson-Pearson, George S. Johnson, Richard Jorgensen, Paul Larsen, Susan Leithe, Linda Nelson, Ronald Peterson, Jeffrey Rohr, William A. Smith, Paul Sponheim, and Theodore Vinger.

Special thanks goes to Herbert W. Chilstrom, former bishop of the Evangelical Lutheran Church in America; to Ronald Klug and James Satter of Augsburg Fortress Publishers for their help through the process; to Lois Anderson for her skill and patience in preparing five drafts of the manuscript; and to Carol, my marital partner since seminary days, to whom I dedicate this book.

LOWELL O. ERDAHL

1

Life-Giving Pastors
Live by the Grace of God

"But by the grace of God I am what I am, and his grace toward me has not been in vain. On the contrary, I worked harder than any of them—though it was not I but the grace of God that is with me" (1 Corinthians 15:10).

Imagine two pastors: One is highly skilled theologically, has an outstanding academic record, has done graduate study beyond seminary, does exegesis in Greek and Hebrew, and is highly regarded as a counselor and preacher. This pastor believes in the doctrine of justification by grace through faith and can lecture well on the subject, but in spite of that intellectual belief and personal confession, really doesn't live by that grace but instead by professional competence. There is no conscious hypocrisy. This pastor is a sincere and well-meaning teacher of biblical truth but, because it is a reality beyond present experience,cannot bear personal witness to what it means to live by the grace of God.

The second pastor is less professionally competent, struggled to get through the seminary, was never acclaimed for academic excellence or theological profundity, but *does* have profound insight into living by the grace of God. Because this pastor knows first-hand what it is to be welcomed by the mercy and strengthened by the power of God, all that this pastor says and does is shaped by and expresses God's life-giving grace.

Suppose that you are on a congregational search committee and have just interviewed these two candidates for a call to your parish. Whom would you choose—the theological expert lacking personal experience of life in grace or the less theologically competent person who really lives by the grace of God?

Depending on the degree of difference between the two candidates, it could be an agonizing choice. As a member of such a search committee,

I would be grateful that each pastor has something significant to offer. Both would be preferable to a pastor with neither theological expertise nor personal experience of grace, but that would not be a comforting consolation. After interviewing such candidates, search committee members would likely ask, "Isn't there someone else? Isn't there a candidate with both theological expertise and personal understanding of and appreciation for the gospel of grace?" Indeed, they might wonder why candidates without those qualities were approved for ordination or permitted to remain in the ministry.

After years of involvement with the certification process, I appreciate the difficulties involved in rejecting persons committed to ministry. Since academic achievement is more easily evaluated than spiritual formation, top students who know the right answers but who lack personal insight born of living by grace are usually affirmed. Those with marginal academic records but profound personal experience of life in grace often receive more scrutiny but are usually certified. Knowing that God uses limited and fallible people like ourselves restrains us from rejecting others.

As a bishop, I also learned how difficult it is to be helpful to clergy who are marginally competent and/or lack personal insight into life-giving grace. We shun confrontation and often fear that intervention may crush a fragile spirit and only makes things worse. It is especially difficult to be helpful when the pastor seems unaware of those limitations and blames every problem on others.

WE NEED NOT STAY AS WE ARE

Yet, if the Christian message means anything, it means that none of us needs stay as we are. We can learn and grow. To minister meaningfully over the long haul, pastors must be both professionally competent and personally sustained by the grace of God. Chapter 4 focuses on lifelong learning and suggests ways of increasing professional competence. This chapter centers on the person more than the professional, more on living by grace than on its theological articulation or pastoral application.

John Wesley risked his life as a missionary long before his "heart was strangely warmed" by the message of grace at Aldersgate, and I once heard of a bishop who was converted at age eighty. There is hope even for bishops!

I hope there have been glimpses of grace in each of our lives. At best, we are only beginners in the adventure of living by the grace of God and need continual renewal in that new life. E. Stanley Jones, a Methodist missionary to India, said that "each of us needs to be converted at least once a year just on general principles."[1] For Martin Luther, once a year was not enough; he taught that baptism means a continuous conversion in which the old self dies every day and a new self is raised up to walk in newness of life. If there have been at least some such days in our pilgrimage, we can gratefully recall times of personally glimpsing the grace of God. To evoke memories of your encounters of grace, I will share some of my own.

PERSONAL GLIMPSES OF GRACE AS MERCY

My first memories of theological reflection and existential doubt are from early childhood. I was taught that God created everything, and I vividly recall the fear that struck me when I wondered, "Where did God come from?" The answer that God did not come from anywhere but instead had always been and would always be evoked a sense of awe and mystery—but it didn't relieve my uncertainty and anxiety.

During confirmation instruction I knew that I was going to be asked to affirm a creedal confession of faith, and I tried hard to talk myself into believing it. Our pastor was kind and compassionate, but I never dared tell him of my doubts. With strong-willed determination I made my confession and was confirmed.

In retrospect, I see that I then understood faith to be believing certain things to be true. I was taught that faith involved "knowledge, assent, and trust," and I had the impression that faith developed in that order. After having been given knowledge of Christian truth, I had first to assent by believing it and could then trust that it was true for me. Such a rationalistic understanding now strikes me as false and misleading.

One of the most grace-filled experiences of late adolescence, and of my entire life, was reading E. Stanley Jones's book *The Way.* Mother had received it from "Grandma Harvey," who was not our grandmother. She was the widow of a Methodist pastor and an admirer of Jones. Having nothing better to do, I began reading the book and discovered that it spoke to my condition. I still remember coming to a page that invited me to "cease from struggling." And when Jones said, "As long as you are trying you are still depending on yourself," I realized he was describing me. When he went on to say, "When I gave all trying over, simply trusting, I was blessed," I began to have a faint perception that faith was not a matter of believing certain things to be true, but rather of letting go and resting my life in God's promised gracious presence. After completing *The Way*, I read many of "Brother Stanley's" devotionals and other writings, and I heard him speak at several ashrams, as his retreat conferences were called. At one of them he autographed my copy of *The Way*, and in tribute to his influence in my life I dedicated my devotional book, *Authentic Living*, to his memory.[2]

While attending St. Olaf, a Christian liberal arts college in Northfield, Minnesota, I hoped to find answers to my continuing doubts and questions. But every answer seemed to raise more questions and doubts, and there were times when I wondered if I believed anything. Then late one night, a line from Luther's explanation to the third article of the Apostles' Creed surfaced in memory—"I believe that I cannot by my own reason or strength believe in Jesus Christ my Lord or come to him." This, I thought to myself, is something I can believe! I realized that I could not by my own understanding or effort believe in Jesus Christ. Nor could I believe everything else that I thought we were required to believe in order to be Christians. Then came the thought, "If God is to have anything to do with me, he will have to take me as I am, not only with all my sins and peculiarities, but also with all of my doubts and questions, perplexities and uncertainties." At that moment it was as if a light went on in my head, and my next thought was, "That's what the gospel says! God takes us just as we are!"

I had sung it many times in church but never really taken it in— "Just as I am thou wilt receive. Wilt welcome, pardon, cleanse, relieve." I had even sung that third stanza that spoke most clearly to my need and which has become a treasure to me:

> Just as I am, though tossed about,
> With many a conflict, many a doubt.
> Fighting and fears within, without.
> O Lamb of God, I come, I come.

This was an example of what Paul Tillich called being "struck by grace." Years later, when I heard Tillich tell of the release and freedom that came into his life when he realized that we are justified in our doubt as well as in our sin, memories of that college night again came to mind. I still find myself in Tillich's beautiful and moving description of an encounter with grace:

> Grace strikes us when we are in great pain and restlessness. It strikes us when we walk through the dark valley of a meaningless and empty life. It strikes us when we feel that our separation is deeper than usual, because we have violated another life, a life which we loved, or from which we were estranged. It strikes us when our disgust for our own being, our indifference, our weakness, our hostility, and our lack of direction and composure have become intolerable to us. It strikes us when, year after year, the longed-for perfection of life does not appear, when the old compulsions reign within us as they have for decades, when despair destroys all joy and courage. Sometimes at that moment a wave of light breaks into our darkness and it is as though a voice were saying: "You are accepted. You are accepted. Accepted by that which is greater than you, the name of which you do not know. Do not ask for the name now; perhaps you will find it later. Do not try to do anything now; perhaps later you will do much. Do not seek for anything; do not perform anything; do not intend anything. Simply accept the fact that you are accepted!" If that happens to us, we experience grace. After such an experience we may not be better than before, and we may not believe more than before. But everything is transformed. In that moment, grace conquers sin, and reconciliation bridges the gulf of estrangement.[3]

I know that grace can strike us when we are on mountain tops of joy as well as "when we walk through the dark valley of a meaningless and empty life," but these words from Tillich are still some of the clearest expressions of justification by grace through faith that I have read.

George Aus, one of my seminary professors, gave me a glimpse of grace when he said, "Just as we shouldn't be so proud as to think we have no sins, so also we should not be so proud as to think our sins are too big for God to forgive." There is certainly arrogance in thinking we have no sins, but there is also false pride in thinking that our sins are too big for God's mercy.

Similarly, grace struck me in Luther's response to a troubled sinner who believed that God was merciful, but not merciful enough to forgive his terrible sins. Luther replied that such thinking was not the voice of God or Christian conscience but instead came from the devil. Luther recommended that if such doubts returned, the person should say, "Devil, you have convicted me of only a few of my little sins. I have sins much worse than any you have mentioned and God knows them all and still loves and forgives me." When Luther gave that assurance he was not minimizing sin but was emphasizing with the apostle Paul that "Where sin increased, grace abounded all the more" (Romans 5:20).

The British preacher Charles Spurgeon gave me a grace moment when he wrote of wondering if God had grace enough to forgive all his awful sins. He went on to tell of how, in imagination, he saw a little fish going to the wise old fish, who was lord of the deep, and saying, "I have decided to drink the sea." To which the wise old fish replied, "That's fine. There is enough for you!" With that image, Spurgeon was assured that with God there is mercy as abounding as the vastness of the sea and was again enabled to trust in the full and complete forgiveness of all his sins.

Grace abounded for me when I heard Luther Seminary professor James Burtness preach a Lenten sermon in my first parish on "Christ, the Mediator of a New Covenant," That covenant, he said, means "Nothing we have ever done or can ever do will stop God from loving us." He reminded us, "We can't stop God from loving us any more than we can stop the sun from shining." The sun doesn't shine because we are nice; it shines because that's the way the sun is. God doesn't love us because we do good things or stop doing bad things, or because we repent and have faith. God loves us because that's the way God is. "God is love" (1 John 4:16). God loves us even more than we love ourselves. Even if we hate and despise ourselves, God still loves us! Living by the grace of God means living by the promise that nothing "in all creation will be able to separate us from the love of God in Christ Jesus our Lord" (Romans 8:39).

17

While saying goodbye after my last worship service at my first parish, a member named Herman Olson asked, "Do you know what is the most important thing you have told us in your ten years as our pastor?"

"No," I replied, "What is that?"

"You told us that nothing we have ever done or can ever do will stop God from loving us."

I again credited that line to Dr. Burtness and today am still grateful to be remembered for sharing that clear expression of the grace by which we live.

Cheap Grace

By now some readers must be thinking, "Isn't this the same kind of 'cheap grace' that Dietrich Bonhoeffer warned us against?" Hearing of abounding grace some may think, "God loves to forgive and I love to sin, so we get along just fine." A temptation toward such thinking is always present when grace is clearly proclaimed, but I think we have to risk it. When the apostle Paul affirmed God's over-abounding grace, some apparently wondered, "Should we continue in sin in order that grace may abound?" To which Paul replied, "By no means! How can we who died to sin go on living in it?" (Romans 6:1-2).

To avoid preaching cheap grace, some proclaim *conditional grace*, which is not grace at all. It's only another form of work righteousness that turns us back toward more self-centered struggling and deeper dependence upon ourselves. God does not love us because we repent; we can repent because God loves us. God does not love us because we have faith; we can have faith because God loves us. Faith is born of the gospel. We are not saved because of our faith. God does not promise to help us save ourselves, but the gracious God we know in Christ does promise to save us without our help.

By Grace, through Faith

Lutherans often talk about "justification by faith." But as I remember my misunderstanding of that phrase and think of the confusion it's caused for many people I have known, I believe we should instead speak of "justification by grace through faith" (Ephesians 2:8). Faith is not something we do to merit God's mercy. Luther spoke of it as "pure passivity." Faith means becoming passive to God's action. It is "letting God be God." It is letting God do everything God has promised to do in Christ.

Suppose I was saved from drowning by a lifeguard. It would be nonsense for me to boast that I was saved by my faith. I would be grateful for having ceased struggling when the lifeguard reached me, rather than frantically trying to save myself. My continued struggle would have hindered, and perhaps even prevented, my rescue. But while yielding welcomed my deliverance, it did not save me. I was saved by the lifeguard! It was welcoming of my rescue but certainly was nothing to boast about. If I were to boast, I should boast of the lifeguard. So also, "Let the one who boasts, boast in the Lord" (1 Corinthians 1:31 and 2 Corinthians 10:17).

When we rest back in the arms of God, we are grateful for grace and no longer proud of our faith. Then we know that grace is neither cheap nor conditional, but costly. We see that cost in the cross, which witnesses to what happens when love meets sin and keeps on loving. "That cross," as E. Stanley Jones often said, "stood not only on the hill at Calvary—it stands eternally in the heart of God," who loves us now in our sin and doubt and promises to love us forever. To live by grace is to rest our lives in that love, trusting that we are held by love that will never let us go and never let us down.

Grace as Power

But there is more to living by grace than resting in God's love. Grace, as Reinhold Niebuhr emphasized long ago, is not only the mercy of God toward us, it is also the power of God at work with us and within us.[4] The great word of assurance that came to the apostle Paul, "My grace is sufficient for you," was not an assurance of mercy sufficient for his forgiveness, but of power sufficient to be his strength in times of weakness (2 Corinthians 12:9-10). For the apostle Paul, living by grace meant living by both the love and power of God. So also for us, grace is not only merciful, forgiving, welcoming, embracing, life-giving love; grace is also sustaining, healing, transforming, enabling, life-giving power.

This means that faith is also more than dependent trust. I believe that Martin Luther was right in describing faith in relation to the grace of mercy as "pure passivity," and that E. Stanley Jones was right in describing faith in relation to the grace of power as "pure receptivity." In the surrender of faith we not only rest in the love of God but also open our lives to welcome the empowering Spirit of God. The promise that you will receive power "when the Holy Spirit has come upon you" (Acts 1:8) witnesses as directly to the grace of God as do the promises of God's forgiveness and mercy.

Lest there be misunderstanding, I should underscore the fact that when surrendered to God we surrender to no one else! Surrender to others diminishes the self; surrender to God is a homecoming that fulfills self. Total dependence upon another person is life-diminishing dependency; total dependence upon God is life-fulfilling liberation. When the false god of self bows down in surrender to the true God of grace, a new authentically human self arises to stand tall before the tyrants that would subdue and enslave us saying, with Luther, "Here I stand. I can do no other. So help me God."

PERSONAL GLIMPSES OF GRACE AS POWER

To evoke your memories of glimpses of grace as the power of God I will again share some memories of my own. Grace as the power of God is significant for me because of what seems to have been a life-long sense of weakness and limitation. More than thirty years ago David Belgum, my supervisor in clinical pastoral education, told me, "You have a low sense of self-worth." If that's true, I am sure it had its beginnings in my childhood experiences with polio and stuttering. Both were then a great embarrassment for me. I recall being upset and angry when other children asked, "Why do you limp?" Or, "How come you stutter?"

When, years later, our youngest daughter referred to "your chicken leg" (because it is so thin), I could laugh about it. But if a kid had made such a comment during my school years, I wouldn't have found it humorous. After years of silent shame I was finally able to talk about my stuttering, which not only relieved my embarrassment but proved to be tremendously therapeutic. Since "stuttering is what people do to keep from stuttering," talking about it helped free me from having to speak fluently, and I am thankful that (except for occasional blocks that remind me that I am still a stutterer) it long ago ceased to be a serious problem. Nevertheless, my "inner child of the past," with all of his feelings and fears, is still within me as a continual reminder of my frailty. I agree with Paul Tournier, author of *The Strong and the Weak*, that this distinction as "a great illusion":

> I believe there is a great illusion underlying both the despair of the weak and the unease of the strong—and the misfortune of both. This great illusion is the very notion that there are two kinds of human beings, the strong and the weak.

> The truth is that human beings are much more alike than they think. What is different is the external mask, sparkling or disagreeable, their outward reaction, strong or weak. These appearances, however, hide an identical inner personality. The external mask, the outward reaction, deceive everybody, the strong as well as the weak. All . . . , in fact, are weak. All are weak because all are afraid. They are afraid of being trampled underfoot. They are all afraid of the inner weakness being discovered. They all have secret faults; they all have a bad conscience on account of certain acts which they would like to keep covered up. They are all afraid of other men and of God, of themselves, of life, and of death.[5]

Although we certainly look and act differently, we are pretty much alike on the inside. We are all vulnerable. Your specific memories of weakness may have little in common with mine, but we have kinship with one another in our weakness.

If life doesn't confront us with our finitude, we can hardly escape it when confronted with death. My memories again go back to childhood. Once when I was very young, my mother observed while putting me to bed that I was crying and asked what was troubling me. I answered, "I'll tell you some day." I am sure I never told her, but I remember what prompted those tears: I was thinking of how we were all going to die— Mom, Dad, my brother, aunts and uncles, neighbors and friends, our dogs and cats, and cattle, pigs and chickens—we were all going to die! I was grieving for them and for me. Some of those creatures didn't know they had to die, but I knew it, and that knowledge evoked a great sadness that moved me to tears. In times like that I know that Tournier is right: The very notion that there are two kinds of human beings, the strong and the weak, is a great illusion.

Life sometimes seems to be like the mantle of the Aladdin's lamp we had back on the farm and like the mantles of Coleman lanterns we used while camping—glowing brightly but exceedingly fragile. The wing of a moth could put out the light and turn the mantle to dust. Maybe I'm morbid, or perhaps the thought of how "the days of our life . . . are soon gone, and we fly away" (Psalm 90:10) was so dinned into me that I have lived with an almost constant sense of the brevity of life. I often think of the sign over a cemetery gate that speaks from the dead to us who live: "What you are, we were. What we are, you will be." The melancholy realism of Thomas Gray's elegy speaks of and to us all:

> The boast of heraldry, the pomp of power,
> And all that beauty, all that wealth e'er gave,
> Awaits alike the inevitable hour,
> The paths of glory lead but to the grave.[6]

When life and death confront us with our weakness and finitude, we may begin to understand and to appreciate as never before the gospel of grace as power. Then, when we are at the end of our resources and there is nothing more for us to do or say, we can still trust in the promises and power of God. In our trembling vulnerability we, like the apostle Paul, live by this promise: "My grace is sufficient for you, for my power is made perfect in weakness" (2 Corinthians 12:9). When death haunts us, we are assured in Christ that "neither death, nor life, . . . nor things present, nor things to come, . . . nor anything else in all creation, will be able to separate us from the love of God in Christ Jesus our Lord" (Romans 8:37-39). That kind of love is not just mercy, but power—power stronger than death; life-giving power. To live by God's grace is not only to rest our lives in the welcome of God's forgiving embrace, but to depend upon a loving power beyond ourselves that enables us to say with the apostle Paul, "I can do all things through him who strengthens me" (Philippians 4:13).

GLIMPSES OF GRACE IN OTHER LIVES

As I am grateful for the grace of mercy and power that has welcomed and sustained me across the years. I also thank God for the glimpses of grace seen in the lives of others. My life has been blessed by dozens of people who have been nothing less than living "means of grace." My predecessor bishop, Elmo Agrimson, called them "walking sacraments." To them I say, "Thank you." Of them I say, "Thanks be to God."

I am specifically grateful for the transformed lives of people in Alcoholics Anonymous and other Twelve Step programs who provide dramatic illustration of what can happen when we live by merciful, powerful grace. Like the apostle Paul, they acknowledge their powerlessness and find their hope in a power beyond themselves. Their surrender involves both trust and receptivity. They rely not only on a gracious welcome into a new relationship but also on an in-dwelling power that enables sobriety and sanity. I have observed that some of those people involved in Twelve Step programs who aren't active in the church seem to have more profound personal understanding of what it is to really live by the grace of God than do many of us churchgoers. Our theology may be better but our lives poorer. They may need theological education concerning the doctrine of grace; we may need more profound experience of living by grace. Some of us may even be like a person who has written a doctoral dissertation meticulously describing the strokes of championship swimming but who never gets in the water. Whatever their theology, many people in Twelve Step groups are, as it were, "swimming in grace" and know what it is to be utterly dependent on a gracious God for sane and sober living. To be long-term, life-giving pastors without accumulated fatigue and eventual burnout, we need a similar experience of daily living by the grace of God.

Whatever the state of our lives, there is still hope for us. "We are not promised," as Julian of Norwich put it, "that we will never be distressed or never be troubled; but we have been promised that we will never be overcome." As one common expression says, "The will of God will not lead us where the grace of God will not keep us." Nor are we promised all the "gifts" of the Spirit (1 Corinthians 12:4-11). Each of those gifts is only for some. But we are all promised all of the "fruit of the Spirit," beginning with love and ending with self-control (Galatians 5:22).

These qualities—love, joy, peace, patience, kindness, generosity, faithfulness, gentleness and self-control—are not the result of our struggle and striving. They are the result of the healing, transforming power of the Spirit of God at work within our lives, and even within the troubled corners of our subconscious minds beyond our awareness. It may also be significant that self-control comes at the end and not the beginning of the list. This is another reminder that these qualities, which are really Christ-like characteristics, are not achieved through our mastery of self-control, but are received in the surrender of passive, receptive faith that lives by the grace of God.

THE OTHER SIDE

Lest all this be misunderstood, I underscore the fact that resting in and receiving the grace of God is only one side of the Christian life. The whole way of life for the Christian person, said Luther, consists in two things: 1) faith in God, and 2) love of neighbor. While emphasizing the passivity of faith, Luther also affirmed the activity of love. Similarly, E. Stanley Jones, who emphasized the receptivity of faith, said that after having "let go and let God," we should go on to say, "Let's go! Let's get busy doing the work Christ sends us to do!"

When asked the secret of his lifelong vitality, Jones once answered that it came from having jobs too big for him to do alone and that this drove him to daily dependence on grace. On another occasion he gave the credit primarily to "grace and gumption." The apostle Paul witnessed to that same combination when he said, "By the grace of God I am what I am, and his grace toward me has not been in vain. On the contrary, I worked harder than any of them—though it was not I, but the grace of God that is with me" (1 Corinthians 15:10), and again, "For this I toil, striving with all the energy which he mightily inspires within me" (Colossians 1:29 RSV). Energy inspired within—that's grace. Toiling and striving by that energy—that's gumption.

Honesty sometimes compels us to confess that we are living with little of either grace or gumption—at other times with much gumption but little grace, and perhaps on occasion with much grace and little gumption. When properly in tune with God and ourselves, we live with both grace and gumption. Passive and receptive in faith, we are busy and active with love. We live like an ocean liner, resting and working at the same time. We let down the weight of our sins and cares on God's mercy and power, resting in grace as the ship rests in the sea. But that ship is not a cork! While at rest in the sea, its engines are powerfully at work, not to lift itself, but to fulfill the purpose for which it was built by carrying passengers and cargo across the ocean. We too work, not to win Christ's love for ourselves, for we are already at rest in that love. We work to share Christ's love with others. "We love because he first loved us" (1 John 4:19).

There were no lakes nor swimming pools near the farm where I grew up and I didn't learn to swim until I was nearly thirty years old. By that time I feared deep water and was convinced that it wanted to pull me down. But I made a great discovery—the water wanted to hold me up! It was my friend and not my enemy! That discovery was the beginning of years of delightful swimming.

In a similar but far more significant way, it is a great day when we discover that the heart of the universe is gracious and that God wants to hold us up, not pull us down. Then we begin not just to believe about grace but to live by grace! Freed from having to struggle to lift ourselves up, we let go and let God's love hold us. Resting in that love, we are free to forget ourselves and, by gracious energy God "mightily inspires" within us, work to fulfill the life-giving ministry that is ours in Christ.

2

Life-Giving Pastors
Bond with Their People

"I thank my God in all my remembrance of you, always in every prayer of mine for you all making my prayer with joy, thankful for your partnership in the gospel from the first day until now. And I am sure that he who began a good work in you will bring it to completion at the day of Jesus Christ. It is right for me to feel thus about you all, because I hold you in my heart, for you are all partakers with me of grace . . ." (Philippians 1:3-7 RSV).

Reinhold Niebuhr told a story about a pastor in the South during the civil rights movement that illustrates an essential habit of life-giving clergy. This pastor was a courageous advocate of racial integration, but for his zeal was rewarded with resentment from many people in the congregation. Some began circulating a petition to get rid of him. When the petitioners invited one elderly gentleman to sign the petition, they were surprised when he refused. "Why won't you sign it?" they asked. "You certainly don't agree with all this integration business?"

"That's right," he said. "But you are forgetting something,"

"What's that?" they asked.

"You are forgetting that my wife died six months ago, and he was, and is, my pastor!"

There are many ways of describing what held that parishioner and pastor together even though their convictions on a specific issue were far apart. To sum it up with one word, they were bonded with each other. Through shared experience during a time of sickness and death, the pastor and parishioner experienced bonding.

Bonding is that something that enabled that parishioner to say, "He was, and is, my pastor." Parishioners who affirm someone as "my pastor" are talking about something more than a professional

26

relationship. They are not just acknowledging that John Smith or Mary Jones is the clergyperson serving the congregation. They are saying, "We have a personal relationship of trust and respect. This pastor cares for me and I care for my pastor."

For me, Niebuhr's story illustrates the reality expressed in what I have sometimes called "Erdahl's Law":

> When pastor and people are well-bonded, the pastor can get away with almost everything. When pastor and people are not well bonded, the pastor can get away with hardly anything.

Well-bonded pastors can make lots of mistakes and express many unpopular opinions and yet still do life-giving ministry. Poorly-bonded pastors, on the other hand, are continually criticized for every foible and are frustrated at every turn. Every deficiency and idiosyncrasy becomes a cause for complaint. Even if not devoured by those who some call "alligators," the picky-picky complaining may become so intolerable that the pastor feels like someone being nibbled to death by ducks.

SAD STORIES TO TELL

One of my saddest experiences as a parish pastor was working with couples with whom the bonding of marriage had broken down. I recall visiting with a woman who told me, "I've decided to get a divorce."

"What prompts you to do that?" I asked.[1]

"I read your *Be Good to Each Other* book," she said.

Surprised, I asked, "What in that book prompts you to get a divorce?"

She replied, "If what you and your wife have written about is marriage, my husband and I haven't had a marriage for over twenty years!" While still legally married, the bonding essential to life-giving marriage was long gone.

In a similar way one of the saddest things I've had to deal with as a bishop is to listen to people tell me that the person serving their congregation "is not my pastor!" They may say that he or she "seems to be pastor to some of the people, but not to me" and often report that if they had a problem they would never go to this person. Their church attendance and contributions decline and they often worship elsewhere or via radio and television services. I have even heard some say, "If I get sick, I don't want a pastoral visit. If I die, I want someone else to conduct the funeral."

If even a small minority of the congregation—5 or 10 percent— have such feelings, the pastor and the congregation have a significant problem. It is especially serious if the pastor has failed to bond with some of the congregation's most active and supportive members.

Failure to bond is rarely the fault of the pastor alone. As with marriage, it takes two to tango and to tangle. Parishioners can, for example, continue to be so tightly bonded with a previous pastor that they don't give the new pastor a chance to bond with them.

Well-established bonding can also be broken. Things can happen on either side that undermine the relationship. Resentment can replace respect, and cooperative support can give way to withdrawal and hostility.

When bonding doesn't happen or is broken, we pastors are often tempted to blame the "alligators" and "clergy-killers." Although they may be at fault and we may be innocent of significant offense, as with all human relationships it is unlikely that all virtue is on one side and all villainy on the other.

If we feel we are being crucified with Jesus, we should remember that there were three crosses on that hill. Chances are probably two-to-one that we are being "nailed" not for our Christ-likeness but, like those thieves, for our sins. "If possible," says the apostle Paul, "so far as it depends on you, live peaceably with all" (Romans 12:18). Therefore, we focus on ourselves, not on the sins of others, and seek to do all that we can do to establish and sustain positive bonding.

HABITS THAT CREATE AND SUSTAIN BONDING

The factors that create and sustain positive human relationships are so complex and diverse that no simple formula can capture and express them all. But to provide a framework for discussion, I will risk oversimplification and suggest that well-bonded pastors live out the following equation:

RESPECT + COMPASSION + COMPETENCE + TIME = BONDING

We will consider each of these components in turn.

Respect

I was tempted to write only "Compassion + Competence + Time = Bonding," but quickly realized that compassion without respect is condescending. If we are to be truly bonded, it is not enough that we feel compassion toward our people. We must also respect them.

After several counseling sessions, a troubled woman with painful physical and emotional problems thanked me and said, "I never felt that you were looking down on me." I was both surprised and gratified by her comment. Why should I look down on her? We were in the struggle of life together. She honored me by sharing her story and her suffering. We were meeting at the foot of the cross, where the ground is level and where no one has a perch from which to look down on anyone else.

When a senior pastor encouraged a new associate to stop in and visit with a group of elderly women meeting at the church, the young pastor replied, "I don't have time to spend with them." To which the senior pastor replied, "You should not only take time, but when you are there, you should take off your shoes because you are standing on holy ground." They were elderly and some were frail, but those women had each earned the equivalent of a Ph.D. in the school of life's joys and sorrows, and they were worthy of time and respect.

Although we pastors may have the best theological education in the congregation (though we dare not assume that to be true) it is unlikely that we are the most insightful, faithful, and loving. Some were sustained by the grace of God long before we heard of it and have profound experience in Christian living. I thank God for the instruction of many wise and learned professors, but I am no less grateful for the wisdom of ordinary people by whom I have been taught and from whom I have gained new perspectives that have shaped my life.

"That's well and good," you may be thinking, "but how am I to have respect for people who have no respect for me? They speak of my predecessors as if they did no wrong and are cool toward me and resistant to my leadership. How can I respect such people?" To this I can only reply, "Very carefully and with a long-term perspective." Early in my time with my first congregation, I was less than pleased to hear people brag about my predecessors and took delight when I heard them criticized. But before long I discovered that those who were most critical of my predecessors were now criticizing me and that those who were most grateful for their past ministries were now among my strongest supporters. This helped me be less troubled by the commendations and less delighted by the condemnations of my predecessors.

Although there are certainly differences among people and congregations, I find it helpful to remember a story told by Pastor Elmer Hjortland:

> A family moving into a new community stops at a gas station and asks, "What kind of town is this?"
>
> "What kind of town do you come from?" replies the station attendant.
>
> "It's a wonderful town," the family responds. "We left some of the kindest and best people we have ever known. Leaving that community has been a great grief for us."
>
> "Well," says the attendant, "that sounds like our town. I am sure you will soon have a lot of new friends and that you will enjoy living here."
>
> A bit later another car stops at the same gas station. These newcomers ask, "What kind of town is this?"
>
> To which the attendant again replies, "What kind of town do you come from?"
>
> "It was cold and friendless," responds the new family. "We were glad to leave that place."
>
> "Well," replied the attendant, "I hate to tell you but that sounds a lot like this place. I think you will find it as cold and friendless as the town you just left."

When we have trouble respecting some of our people, the fault may not be in the congregation, but in ourselves. There may be some "alligators" and "clergy-killers" who are hard to respect, but before condemning them we need to examine ourselves to see if there is anything in us that is evoking this response. When I take an honest look at myself, I sometimes discover a "log" in my eye that is hindering my ability to "see" clearly enough to take the speck out of my could be a lot worse. But even that small percentage reveals a big problem! A bishop with 200 active pastors will not be cheered by news that only eight are incompetent! And, if Rediger is right, what does his estimate imply concerning the number who are marginally competent and often ineffective?

Since almost everything in this book encourages habits that create competence, I will not belabor the issue. Suffice it to say that when incompetence or marginal competence is the basic problem, it must either be corrected to enable bonding and effective, life-giving ministry, or the pastor should seek another vocation.

Time

Respect + Compassion + Competence does not instantly yield positive pastor/parishioner bonding. Bonding takes time. When pastors exude respect, compassion, and competence, and the congregation eagerly welcomes and affirms a new pastor, significant bonding may be quickly established, but if there are more than 300 members, it will probably take at least a year.

On my first Sunday as pastor at University Lutheran Church of Hope in Minneapolis, our daughter Becky overheard parishioners visiting after worship. "What do you think of the new pastor?" asked one. "Well," replied another, "I think he will be all right, but it will take a while to get used to him."

When I heard that comment, my first thought was, "I'll settle for that!" It takes time for a congregation to get used to a new pastor and even longer to become positively bonded.

Alvin Rogness offered two contradictory maxims to Luther Seminary seniors who would soon be serving in their first parishes:

1) Don't change anything the first year.

2) If you don't change anything the first year, you will never change anything.

Pastors, young and old, do well to ponder both statements when beginning new ministries. If frustrated with a slow-moving congregation and tempted to create change by coercion and manipulation, we

neighbor's eye (Luke 6:42). When that log is removed, I have a better view of the people who are giving me trouble and have even discovered qualities in their lives that evoke respect.

Compassion

We all suffer in many ways, and those who are hurting the most may be in such denial that they don't admit it even to themselves. When frustrated by people with whom it is difficult to bond we wisely remember the old Native American wisdom: "Do not criticize others until you have walked at least a mile in their moccasins." When we are really attentive, we no longer react only to other people's expressions of negative feelings but also to their inner pain and suffering. This doesn't resolve all interpersonal conflict, but it helps evoke and sustain compassion.

In *Be Good to Each Other*, we tell of a married couple who are having an intense argument. The angry wife was vicious in berating her husband. When the counselor asked, "What are you trying to tell him?" her mood changed and she began to cry. Through her tears she blurted out, "I just wish that he'd take me in his arms and tell me that he loves me." It is unlikely that the husband was getting that message! All that he heard was anger and resentment, yet all the while she was pleading for assurance of his love.

In parish ministry, as in marriage, we need to listen to the sounds of the heart, as well as the angry words, and look behind hostile actions to the inner anguish that may be prompting them. When we do so, we often discover some goodness behind the expression of things that look evil. Angry words and hurtful behavior may be acts of desperation that rise from God-given, but frustrated, yearnings for love.

We wish from others the empathy that enables them to respond to our inner pain and not just to our impulsive expressions of anger and frustration. In faithfulness to the Golden Rule and the compassion of Christ, we seek similar empathy toward others. By the grace of God some have grown in gentleness and gratitude in the midst of suffering, while in others, suffering has created resentment and bitterness. All of us sometimes, and some of us most times, may be among those A. E. Housman called "too unhappy to be kind."

> . . . these are not in plight to bear
> If they would another's care.
> They have enough as 'tis: I see
> In many an eye that measures me
> The mortal sickness of a mind
> Too unhappy to be kind.
> Undone with misery, all they can
> Is to hate their fellow man;
> Until they drop they need must still
> Look at you and wish you ill.[2]

Happy people can also be unkind, but Housman witnesses to a truth worth remembering: meanness often springs from misery. J. B. Phillips translates the beatitude, "Happy are the kind-hearted" (Matthew 5:7). Kindness creates happiness, happiness also creates kindness. Remembering that we are often unkind when miserable helps us have empathetic compassion toward those who are unkind to us.

It is especially difficult to empathize with those whose experiences are remote from our own. How do the healthy really empathize with the sick? The young with the old? The joyful with the sad? When teaching at Luther Seminary, I asked students to tell of their experiences with loss and grief, and I was surprised to learn that some had never attended a funeral. Such people can rightly thank God for lives free from grief, but what are they to say to people crushed by tragic loss? They certainly can't say, "I know exactly how you feel." But they can say, as all of us must in conversations with those whose experiences are beyond our own, "I'm sure I can't fully understand or feel what you are going through."

When empathy is beyond us, we can still be there with compassion that listens, learns, and cares. In spite of our many differences we are still remarkably alike on the inside. We don't have to live very long before we experience enough joy and enough pain to have much common ground even with those with whom we have many differences.

When our experiences are similar, it is often an expression of empathetic compassion to share them. When someone tells me of traumatic childhood hospitalization, stuttering, or the loss of a baby or parent,

I believe it helpful for me to share a little of my personal expe with similar afflictions and losses. But it would certainly be fooli: hurtful for a pastor to share some things with a parishioner und guise of empathetic compassion. For a pastor to tell a lonely v who has just spoken of her loveless marriage that he knows exact she feels, because there is similar coldness in his marriage, woul best unprofessional and, at worst, seductive.

Meticulous respect for professional boundaries (which we wi sider in chapter nine) should not, however, keep us from being human beings in our pastoral relationships. Years ago, Paul Tc expressed the conviction that we help people more by confessi struggles and difficulties than by boasting of our strengths and ries. Sharing that does not violate boundaries, but acknowledg we are in the struggle of life together, is a vital aspect of the com that creates bonding.

Competence

Respect and compassion create pastoral bonding but cannot s without competence. This is also true of other professions. A car respectful medical doctor or financial adviser, for example, m; quickly with persons seeking guidance. But if the doctor misd and mistreats a serious illness or if the financial adviser recor an investment that results in the loss of life savings, the bond not survive.

Similar stories can be told about pastors. Some bond qui well, but as time passes parishioners become disillusioned. T tell of how much they like the pastor but then go on to compla confusing sermons, poorly prepared Bible studies, and lacklu toral leadership. As parishioners begin to question the pasto ability and wisdom, their trust ebbs away. While they may co: see the pastor as a likeable person, the pastor/parishioner bor been eroded. If the pastor is unable to correct the parishioner: sion of incompetence, positive pastor bonding that enables life-giving ministry cannot be restored.

Clergy and bishops may take heart from Lloyd Rediger's that only 4 percent of pastors are incompetent. If that's tr

should also ponder a line psychiatrist Paul Kerstin once shared with a group of clergy: "We don't make the beans grow by pulling on them!" When confronted with a fruitless tree, the gardener in Jesus' parable advocated a wiser strategy: "Let it alone for one more year, until I dig around it and put manure on it" (Luke 13:8). The fruit-bearing of life-giving ministry, like that of horticulture, more often results from patient digging and fertilization than from anxious manipulation. Edmund H. Friedman emphasized this point when he said:

> To become a leader of a new family, one must become its head. If it is an established family, then one will not emerge as its head through some natural process of that organism's growth. In such a "transplant," time must be allowed for the "graft" to take. In fact, if entering clergy would make this their main priority for the first year or two, rather than hurrying to introduce new programs, not only will they increase their chance of a long-lasting marriage, they are also more likely to see those program ideas accepted.[3]

On the other hand, don't forget Rogness's second maxim:

> If the congregation is, or can quickly become, truly united in favor of significant change, it may be wise to implement it without delay. In any event, it is certainly well to avoid getting locked into the patterns of the past.

BUILD A BONDING BALANCE

Every pastor has, as it were, an account in the "Bank of Parish Influence." Positive bonding puts "money" in the bank. Just as it is unwise to write checks for more money than is in our bank account, it is risky for a pastor to overdraw the bonding balance. When respect, compassion, and competence have built solid bonding over time, the pastor may be able to temporarily overdraw the account in confidence that a "ready reserve" will keep the checks from bouncing. But wise pastors know that most congregations, like most banks, don't provide instant ready reserve accounts to newcomers who have not yet demonstrated their trustworthiness—and staying overdrawn for long can be costly.

In this regard it is significant to note that Martin Luther's reputation as a caring and competent pastor was well-established through his vernacular writings prior to his controversial challenges to the church. Historian Mark Edwards points out that Luther's early pastoral and devotional writings:

> ... laid the foundation for the special charisma that Luther enjoyed, establishing him in the public eye first as an earnest and constructive pastor and man of the Bible, concerned above all for the religious well-being of the laity. Luther made his appearance in the vernacular press as an angry critic of the papacy only after this first impression had been well-established.

> ... The view of Luther as an earnest "man of the Bible" concerned for the spiritual well-being of the laity was well-fixed in the public mind months before Luther's great anti-papal polemics first appeared in the vernacular press.[4]

If possible, we, like Luther, bond with our people before getting involved in potentially divisive controversies.

A FINAL RECOMMENDATION

I close these reflections on bonding with one more suggestion: put positively, Be *vulnerable*; put negatively, *Beware of defensiveness*. Pastoral defensiveness and fear of vulnerability destroy bonding and undermine life-giving ministry. Yet, these characteristics abound among us. I've seen them in myself and in many people with whom I have worked as a bishop. Our situation and our hope are illustrated in Pastor J. W. Stevenson's account of his encounter with a father who had just discovered that his teenage daughter was pregnant:

> He was on the edge of breaking down. That was his hope. He had to break down. The woman in adultery was once more before the Pharisee. This is our human predicament; this is the confusion we are in, that we can scarcely judge evil without increasing the evil in ourselves. . . . I was afraid for this man, as he began to lose grip on

himself—until I saw that it was his grip on himself which held him back from God and from what God wanted him to be.

I was on the instant ready to comfort him and bring him back to himself—until I saw that this was exactly where he must not be brought back. The evil was not in the crumbling of his life but in the shoring of it up, not in the suffering of mind which he was going through but in the desire to escape from the suffering. . . .

Our fears are for the wrong things—fear that our defenses will fall down, when it is our defenses which put us in peril; fear that we may have to be changed, when our wretchedness comes from going on as we are.[5]

In times of confrontation with my personal defensiveness and fear of vulnerability I often think of those lines from Stevenson. When I am at "the edge of breaking down," is that also my hope? Is it really true that "We can scarcely judge evil without increasing the evil in ourselves"? When I point a finger in judgment, do I not only have three fingers pointing back at me but am I actually increasing the evil within me? Does my grip on myself hold me "back from God and from what God [wants me] to be"? Is it true for me and for many of us that "Our fears are for the wrong things—fear that our defenses will fall down, when it is our defenses which put us in peril; fear that we may have to be changed; when our wretchedness comes from going on as we are"?

In troubled situations one pastor says, "It's all their fault" while another asks, "What am I doing wrong?" If you were bishop, with whom would you prefer to deal? To whom would you give the most hopeful prognosis for constructive change? Strong and lasting pastor/parishioner bonding happens when we meet each other as authentic human beings, sharing our gifts and confessing our weaknesses. It happens when we remember that we are in the struggle of life together—equal as sinners and as people loved by God—called in Christ to share "partnership in the gospel from the first day until now" (Philippians 1:5 RSV). Then we can learn in our own experience that "Respect + Compassion + Competence + Time = Bonding." To enable effective, life-giving ministry, may such bonding more and more abound among us.

3

Life-Giving Pastors
Exercise Gift-Evoking Leadership

"A dispute also arose among them as to which one of them was to be regarded as the greatest. But he said to them, 'The kings of the Gentiles lord it over them; and those in authority over them are called benefactors. But not so with you; rather the greatest among you must become like the youngest and the leader like one who serves. For who is greater, the one who is at the table or one who serves? Is it not the one at the table? But I am among you as one who serves.'" (Luke 22:24-27).

"To an extent," says Warren Bennis, "leadership is like beauty: it's hard to define, but you know it when you see it."[1] To test that assertion and to lead into our consideration of leadership, think of occasions when you have witnessed the exercise of pastoral leadership. Please note that I am not asking you to select the people who are the best leaders. That, too, would be an interesting and significant exercise, but it would focus on a few individuals instead of on the occasions, attitudes, and actions that demonstrate leadership by whoever is leading.

What did you see when you searched your memory for examples of pastoral leadership? Did most of your examples come from a few people you would label leaders? Did some come from people who are seldom, if ever, thought of as leaders? How many examples of leadership did you recall from your own experience?

As I try to understand, describe, and encourage parish leadership, I think of a talk given by Mary Schramm who was then exercising leadership at Holden Village, a retreat center in Washington state. Her talk was not about leadership but about gifts. Schramm spoke about "evoking"—calling forth—the gifts of people for ministry and mission. For me, that image of someone evoking gifts for the work and witness of Christ has come to symbolize what is involved in pastoral leadership.

Pastoral leaders evoke the diverse and multitudinous gifts of their parishioners for mission and ministry. This understanding of leadership is similar to that affirmed by Ronald Heifetz in *Leadership Without Easy Answers*. He distinguishes between leadership that means "influencing the community to follow the leaders' vision" and leadership that means "influencing the community to face its problems."[2] More positively, leadership in the Christian community mobilizes people by evoking their gifts for the fulfillment of life and ministry in the service of Christ.

Such gift-evoking, person-mobilizing leadership is soundly grounded in the New Testament understanding of Christian stewardship and is strongly affirmed by the great commissions in Matthew 28:19-20 and Acts 1:8, and the life-giving commission of Acts 5:20 that is the focus of this book.

Because the work of the church is much bigger than work in the church, the evoking of gifts for ministry is not just a call to specific Christian vocations or an invitation to do volunteer church work. Someone told me that he almost screamed out loud during a sermon when his pastor said, "Some people in this congregation are so busy pursuing their careers that they have no time for ministry." Perhaps he should have screamed and then reminded the preacher and congregation that every useful, life-enhancing occupation can be Christian ministry.

As Christian pastors we seek to express the gospel of grace with such clarity that it evokes a response of "faith active in love" (Galatians 5:6). That love involves care and compassion in personal relationships, as well as commitment to justice, which theologian Joseph Sittler described as "love acting at a distance." Pastoral leaders evoke gifts and mobilize people to create welcoming, caring communities for service and mission in the world.

THE SOURCE OF A LEADER'S POWER

The power of leaders comes from the cooperation and support of their people. If you doubt this assertion, recall the experience of leaders like Rehoboam (see 1 Kings 12:1-20), the Shah of Iran, and Ferdinand Marcos of the Philippines, who in spite of great wealth and military power had to flee for their lives. If the power of such potentates depends on the support of their people, how much more so for pastors, who have no power to force church volunteers to do anything.

There have been times when ecclesiastical tyrants could compel obedience by threats of hellfire and damnation, but in most denominations that day is long gone. In fact, some enraged members now seem to feel free to tell the pastor to "go to hell" as they stomp off to find another church! Just as governments can be toppled by civil disobedience, ministries can be destroyed and pastoral careers ended by ecclesiastical disobedience. Examples abound—angry parishioners begin withholding their gifts, then they stop attending worship and resign from volunteer service. If their dissatisfaction persists, they begin voting with their feet; when attempts to reconcile fail, they may transfer their membership to other parishes or become church dropouts. There are almost always some parishioners who continue to affirm the pastor, but if even a sizable minority withdraws support, effective ministry is undermined and sometimes destroyed.

Realism regarding the difficulty of performing effective ministry without strong membership support prompts me to advocate that those congregations that vote to call pastors require a two-thirds vote to call a pastor, a majority vote to remove the pastor with the concurrence of the bishop (district president or comparable regional executive), and a two-thirds vote to remove the pastor over the objection of the bishop. This gives the bishop some power to support a pastor who is being rejected for courageous, prophetic ministry, but it also recognizes the difficulty of ministering effectively when more than half the members want a new pastor.

Because cooperation and support are grounded in trust, it is essential that parish leaders be perceived as people who can be trusted. Trusting is not the result of an act of will. Our trust is created by the people we trust. For example, something has gone terribly wrong if a husband or wife needs to say, "I'm going to try to trust my spouse today." Effective, life-giving ministry, like solid marriage, requires qualities of competence and character that create and sustain such trust. Con artists are adept at creating trust but terrible at sustaining it. Phoniness in close-working relationships is soon found out, and the trust is displaced by a sense of betrayal. Pastor, congregation, and bishop often find it difficult to accept the fact that a clergy person who lacks the ability to evoke trust cannot provide effective congregational leadership.

"THE VISION THING"

Almost everything written on leadership has something to say about "The Vision Thing," as President George Bush called it. Leaders are presented as people of vision who have clear goals for an organization and a passion to motivate the group to reach them. I strongly affirm visionary leaders but believe a warning is in order, especially for pastors serving well-established churches with long histories and habits of their own. If ministry is to be effective in such congregations, the vision must be shared and not imposed by the pastor. In fact, it is best if the vision itself is evoked from the people so they see it as theirs and not just the pastor's.

New pastors may be misled by an enthusiastic search committee that is captivated by the pastor's vision during the interview process and says, "You are just the person we have been waiting for to lead our congregation in exciting new directions." That may be true, but the pastor had better test that vision by listening to the rest of the congregation before trying to impose a new direction. The elected leaders may affirm the pastor's vision and ask for dramatic change, but they may not like it when they see it. Beyond that, they may not represent the views of the unelected leadership and the majority of members who are content with the status quo and committed to maintaining it.

The first step in implementing a new vision is often to find people in the parish who share it and then to get busy planting it in the lives of others so that it can take root and grow. When that happens, a new vision can be evoked from the congregation, with pastor and people working together for its implementation rather than being at odds with one another. If pastor and congregation are to realize a

41

vision, education must often precede implementation. Ronald Heifetz makes this point when he says:

> [T]he task of leadership consists of choreographing and directing learning processes in an organization or community. Progress often demands new ideas and innovation. As well, it often demands changes in people's attitudes and behaviors. Adaptive work consists of the process of discovering and making those changes. Leadership, with or without authority, requires an educative strategy.[3]

We pastors also need to remember that congregations that have heard and lived the gospel long before our arrival contain much wisdom and that some members may have a vision better than our own. In such parishes our opportunity and challenge is to be captured by their vision, and our task is to lead in its implementation. Because we should beware of "always" as well as "never" statements, I doubt that Carl Jung was correct in saying, "The true leader is always led." But I am sure that all true leaders are listeners and learners and that they are often led. Heifetz cites President Lyndon Johnson's crusade for civil rights as an example of such leadership:

> We often think that leadership means having a clear vision and the capacity to persuade people to make it real. In this case, Johnson had authored no vision. Events acted on him to shape the vision to which he then gave powerful articulation. He identified the nation's vision and put it into words. As the nation clarified its values, so did he. Johnson's leadership lay in his wherewithal to give meaning to the crisis and avoid the common pitfall of restoring order prematurely. He let the heat remain high. He kept people's attention on the issues generating the heat. He shifted responsibility to those with the problem. He let the dissident voices be heard. Along with the nation he wrestled with his fundamental orienting values. He gave those values the power of his voice and his presence. He seized the moment to turn the nation's emerging values into potent legislation.[4]

After pondering this example, we ask: Is our challenge and task to impose our vision or to identify the congregation's vision and put it into action? Do we need to let responsibility rest with those who are in crisis rather than taking it on ourselves? Do we need to let dissident voices be heard? Do pastor and parishioners need to wrestle together with fundamental values and to act only when those have been clarified? Do we then provide leadership by giving those values the power of pastoral voice and presence?

Whether the vision comes from the pastor or is discovered and identified within the congregation, its implementation requires ownership by the people of the parish. Remember again that the power of leaders comes from the cooperation and support of their people. When pastor and people affirm a shared vision, great things begin to happen, and changes are effected without divisive, destructive conflict.

LEADERSHIP STYLES

I have observed three dominant leadership styles among pastors. As I describe them, each is really a caricature and not a description of any individual, but they may nevertheless be helpful to our understanding.

Those Who Fail to Exercise Leadership

Pastors who have this first style of leadership really don't lead. Pastors who fail to exercise leadership neither articulate a vision of their own nor capture, express, and mobilize the vision of the congregation. They are drifters not navigators. Many don't act and most fail to even react. They may be at rest in the love of God, but in that rest they have fallen asleep. At best, they get out of the way and enable lay leaders to inspire and guide the congregation. At worse, their lack of leadership results in malaise and stagnation in the parish.

Authoritarian Leaders

At the other extreme are authoritarian pastors. They exercise an imperial and sometimes dictatorial style of leadership. With the apparent blessing of a submissive executive committee, they call the shots and direct the congregation. If they are people of wisdom and compassion, this style can be efficient and effective, at least for a while. It works great when everything is going well and the congregation is happy. But it doesn't work so well in troubled times. When problems arise, the pastor and supportive lay leaders are seen as the villains. Then they wonder, "What went wrong? Everyone seemed joyful and content. But now half the congregation is up in arms!"

The surprised response of such authoritarian leaders indicates that they failed to realize that congregational support is always tentative and conditional. Congregations often give their leaders the benefit of the doubt and, in effect, "let out the rope" to give them leeway to lead. But when the leaders go too far in what many perceive to be the wrong direction, the congregation often pulls back on the rope with such intensity that the pastor is, in effect, thrown out of the saddle!

When pastors and lay leaders ask, "How much change can we make without a vote of the congregation?" my standard reply is, "As much as you can get away with!" This means that pastors and lay leaders had better have a very clear sense of congregational support before attempting innovation without explicit congregational authority. If congregational support is in doubt, the matter should be submitted to a vote. It is far better to have an unnecessary meeting with a unanimous vote of authorization than to have a special meeting later called by protesters seeking to reverse a pastoral or executive committee decision.

Authoritative Leaders

From my perspective, the most effective pastors neither fail to exercise leadership nor are they authoritarian; instead they are authoritative. Their leadership, as the root meaning of the Greek word for authority suggests, is "out of the nature of things"—it grows out of awareness of congregational reality. They fulfill what Max De Pree called "the first responsibility of a leader."[5] And the first responsibility of a leader, De Pree said, "is to define reality." Through careful listening and learning, authoritative leaders understand the people of the parish and have a realistic sense of possibilities and limitations. They neither drift nor dictate. They are continually involved in a process of discerning and developing congregational vision on the one hand and evoking gifts and mobilizing action on the other.

Their leadership style involves neither capitulation nor coercion. They bring people together in support of common goals, whether those be increased support for global missions or a new building program. A minority may dissent and fail to give support, but if bonding is sustained by respectful, compassionate competence, they will usually stay with the parish and not stand in the way of progress.

CONCERNING STAFF AND LAY LEADER RELATIONSHIPS

For the most effective leadership I believe that pastors should heed the wisdom of Stephen Covey, who encourages the boss to be "the first assistant to each of his subordinates."[6] Living out this understanding of staff/volunteer relationships is exceedingly important. It works best when one's staff associates and volunteer colleagues (as I prefer to call them rather than "subordinates") are competent, dedicated people. Wise and secure pastors are not easily threatened by the competence and accomplishments of colleagues. They seek to surround themselves with people as able, and preferably more able, than themselves. Such pastors then serve as their "first assistants" rather than as their dictatorial or detailed directors.

To cite the example I know best, we operated on this principle in our Saint Paul Area Synod staff. Although "Bishop" was on my door and "Assistant to the Bishop" on theirs, I was really the "first assistant" to each of them. Marilyn Breckenridge coordinated the call process, and I was her first assistant. Ron Peterson had central responsibilities for stewardship and outreach, and I was his first assistant. Myrna Sheie was "assistant for administration," and I was her first assistant. She, in turn, was, in effect, the first assistant of each of the support staff. We worked together for eight years, and it was a delight to be colleagues in ministry. I believe this was in large measure the result of our having practiced what Covey advocates.

This required some adjustment on my part. At first, I chaired our staff meetings. But after several weeks, one of our staff was bold enough to suggest that, as assistant for administration, Myrna should assume that responsibility. Although a bit chagrined that my chairing skills were not properly appreciated, I agreed to try it and was blessed with the result. Her carefully prepared agendas, and gentle but firm, guidance of discussion, made for more efficient meetings. Being free from the details of chairing, I could focus on the issues, and this, I believe, increased my ability to contribute to the meetings.

I had a similar experience while serving as senior pastor at University Lutheran Church of Hope in Minneapolis. The senior pastor's report was always near the beginning of board meetings, before the reports and recommendations of a dozen commissions dealing with various areas of the congregation's work and witness. Following one meeting, Charles Bruning, the congregational president, gently informed me that he thought my reports were "stealing the thunder" of the commission chairs and suggested that I give my report after theirs. Although tempted to feel that my visionary leadership was being challenged, I agreed to follow the suggestion and discovered that it worked exceedingly well. I still came to the meetings with my list of concerns, but by the time all chairpeople had reported, most of my concerns had already been discussed and I'd had ample opportunity to comment on each of them. My leadership had not been diminished in the least, while the role of lay leaders had been significantly enhanced. We followed the same procedure during our synod council meetings, and there too I affirm it with gratitude.

Lest these illustrations convey a wrong impression, I should probably confess that I am an ENTJ on the Meyers–Briggs Type Indicator, which puts me in the "field marshall" category. We ENTJs and others with similar characteristics need to balance our commandant tendencies with respectful wisdom that is open to listen to and learn from colleagues and then do all we can to assist them without being threatened by their abilities and accomplishments. When they do the well, we look good!

BE AN ENCOURAGER

We evoke more gifts and mobilize more people by encouraging and affirming them than by complaining and correcting. When correction is needed, we wisely express it as a confession of our thoughts and feelings instead of as a negative judgment on another person's work or character. When expressing positive affirmation, it is fine to start the sentence with "you"—as in, "You did a great job on that project." But when expressing negatives it is better to start with "I"—as in, "I'm sorry you weren't able to complete that project on time." That statement is a confession. To say, "You failed to complete the project," is an accusation and attack. Or to cite another example, it is better to say, "I didn't make myself clear," than to say, "You don't understand what I'm saying." In both examples, the first statement invites conversation and mutual confession, while the second invites counterattacks and conflict.

We should also remember to think in terms of "what's right?" and not of "who's right?" and should encourage others to do the same. When everyone on a church council or other governing group thinks in terms of "who's right?" there is frequent wrangling over whose idea will be implemented. But if everyone is looking for the best idea, creativity without conflict is possible. If others have ideas better than our own, we should be wise enough to recognize and implement them.

When good ideas are suggested and excellent work is done, we should also be honest enough to say, "Thank you." Expressing appreciation and affirmation gives encouragement and strengthens the morale and effectiveness of every organization. It is one of the safest, as well as wisest, things a leader can do. My colleague Ron Peterson was on to something worth remembering when he said, "I've sometimes gotten myself into trouble, but I've never been in trouble for saying 'Thank you.'"

The apostle Paul speaks of the "God of steadfastness and encouragement" (Romans 15:5) and he encourages us to "encourage one another and build up each other as indeed you are doing" (1 Thessalonians 5:11). When I think of people who have lived that verse, I remember my mother, of whom a cousin said on the day of her unexpected death, "She always encouraged me." What a wonderful way to be remembered, and how appropriate for one who lived trusting the "God of steadfastness and encouragement." Wouldn't it be a wonderful world if all of us could be such persons of encouragement!

Our basic business as Christian leaders is to build up, not tear down; to be constructors, not wreckers; to be encouragers, not criticizers; to be affirmers, not complainers; to be life-givers, not life-takers. There are certainly times to confront and correct evil and folly. Jesus did that in his confrontation with self-righteous religious leaders and when he drove the money-changers out of the temple. But it is well to remember that Jesus was most critical of the critics. Jesus' central work was to love and encourage. "Indeed, God did not send the Son into the world to condemn the world, but in order that the world might be saved through him" (John 3:17). It was "the thief" who came "to steal and kill and destroy." Jesus "came that they might have life and have it abundantly" (John 10:10).

The apostle Paul likens himself to "a skilled master builder" (1 Corinthians 3:10). So, too, our primary business is to build up and not tear down. We will always see plenty to complain about, but are to be especially attentive to all that we can honestly affirm and encourage. Someone has suggested that every word of criticism and correction should be balanced by at least seven words of appreciation and affirmation. We may debate those numbers, but I believe the idea is essentially sound.

LEADERSHIP AND MANAGEMENT

It is a mistake to set management and leadership over against each other. We need both. This was brought home to me when an astute observer describing the demise of a leadership institute stated, "What that place needed was some good management!" Leadership without good management can result in chaos. Management without good leadership can result in sterile bureaucracy. Every organization needs both good management and good leadership. We are especially blessed when both qualities are found in the same person.

We do not always succeed, and it is good not to take ourselves too seriously. Everything is not under our control. The church is God's, not ours. We wisely follow the example of the person who began each day by resigning from being chair of the board of the universe.

A group of college presidents were told that they were not to think of themselves as powerful and dynamic leaders but instead as "herders of cats." As pastors, there are times when that image fits our situation. We sometimes seem to have about as much control of our people as would someone trying to herd cats. But if we have a sense of humor and don't take ourselves too seriously, we can still make the best of it.

It isn't always necessary to round up all the cats. We haven't failed as leaders if some refuse to be faithful followers. In fact, as Ronald Heifetz points out, it may be a mistake for us to think of ourselves as leaders with followers. Because so-called "leaders" don't always lead, and because "followers" are sometimes leaders, we should think of "the exercise of leadership" rather than labeling people as either "leaders" or "followers." Heifetz points out that no one would have called Rosa Parks a leader, but at a crucial time in U.S. history she kept her seat in the front of the bus and thereby exercised great leadership. Concerning the use of the word "follower," Heifetz says:

> It seems to me that follower hopelessly entangles us in an inappropriate social contract and logic. Although our common use of language makes us think there is inerrant truth to the couplet leader-follower, just as we do with pairs like up-down and good-bad, I think there is no truth here, merely custom. Indeed, the word follower, which connotes somewhat mindless, lemming-like behavior, fails to suggest how it feels and what it means to be mobilized to do adaptive work. . . . For example, when Martin Luther King, Jr., stimulated white conservative citizens to imagine a different balance of values and power, he led them, and they changed in the process; but they did not follow. They were stimulated to think and feel new thoughts, but they were not in the least his followers. King's black constituents as well were stimulated and empowered to rethink their values, self-images, and habits. However, to call them followers captures not all their role in shaping the process of change in America nor the way they experienced that role.⁷

If we have stimulated people to think better thoughts and to live with more Christ-like attitudes, and if we have evoked their gifts and mobilized their lives for Christian witness and service— if we have inspired them to trust and follow Jesus—then we have succeeded whether they follow us or not. May such gift-evoking and life-mobilizing leadership increasingly enhance the effectiveness of our life-giving ministry.

4

Life-Giving Pastors
Are Lifelong Learners

"If you stop learning, you will forget what your already know"
(Proverbs 19:27 CEV).

"Learn from me." Jesus (Matthew 11:29).

"Do your best to present yourself to God as one approved by him,
a worker who has no need to be ashamed, rightly explaining the
word of truth" (2 Timothy 2:15).

Imagine three lakes: The first has a river running into it, but none that runs out. It receives but does not give. The most famous of such lakes is, no doubt, the Dead Sea. It illustrates what happens when we take but do not give: we stagnate and die.

The second lake has rivers running into it and from it, but the upper river has now been dammed and diverted to a different channel. As a result the level of the lake gradually falls, the stream flowing out is reduced to a trickle, and the lake bed dries up. This lake illustrates what happens when we give without receiving: we dry up and soon have nothing to give.

The third lake has streams running into it and from it. It continually receives and continually gives. Being replenished, it maintains itself even as refreshing waters flow from it to quench the thirst of land and living creatures far beyond itself. This lake illustrate the beauty of life-giving living made possible by lifelong receiving and giving. In Christ we are called to be neither Dead Seas nor dry lake beds, but instead living lakes that welcome rivers of renewal and overflow in streams that bring new life to others.

Life-giving pastors are lifelong learners. Our curiosity invites it and our calling demands it. Because we are less than perfect pastors, aware of partial understanding and limited skills, the fulfillment of our high calling often seems beyond us. Honest recognition of our inadequacies may cause feelings of frustration and distress. But, we need not stay as we are. We are called to be lifelong learners. Learning is a vital part of what pastors are paid to do and we should take time to do it. Will Durant spoke wisdom for pastors when he said, "Learn something every day. Education is not a task, it is a lifelong happiness."[1]

If our job were to shovel sand eight hours a day, we would not need continuing education courses to improve our performance. But if we are to preach meaningfully week after week, inspire youths and adults to noble living, comfort the bereaved, counsel the distressed, reach out and welcome outsiders, be a voice for justice, and lead a community of diverse and sometimes contentious people, we need all the help we can get. After only a few weeks in the parish, we know that our seminary classes, even if excellent, provided only a beginning of education for ministry. Even if we have been diligent students, we often confront complex situations and controversial issues that remind us that we all have something more to learn.

If we are idealistic perfectionists, the challenge to "fulfill the ministry you have received from the Lord" (Colossians 4:17 RSV) may seem overwhelming. When that has happened to me, two mottos have helped enable me to survive. One is "Muddle through," and the other is "Anything worth doing is worth doing poorly." I am not proud of living by those mottos and do not commend them to lazy, careless, or sloppy people. But I do commend them to pastors who live under the tyranny of impossible ideals, so captured by perfectionism that they can hardly do anything. Sometimes, the best we can do is muddle through, and there are many things better done poorly then left undone.

Our subjective evaluation of our own work may also be flawed. The well-known preacher Paul Scherer once told of a person who came to him and said, "You preached a sermon ten years ago that changed my life." He went on with details of time, place, and content that enabled Scherer to check back on that sermon. Across his notes Scherer had written, "This sermon is lousy. Never use it again!" When most proud of ourselves, we may have provided an excellent performance but failed in our ministry; when depressed over seeming failure, a grace event of life-giving significance may have happened in someone's life.

But what if our negative self-evaluation is realistic and we lack the understanding and skills essential for ministry? If that is our impression, we should test it by seeking objective evaluations from people we respect and trust. If they agree that we lack ability for ministry, the only realistic options are to receive education and training that leads to competence or to pursue another vocation.

My greatest concern is not with those who are painfully aware of their limitations but rather with those with such self-deceptive grandiosity that they are unaware of their inability and poor habits that make for ineffective ministry. There is hope for pastors who seek help with preaching, teaching, personal relationship skills, counseling, or whatever. They are open to learn and are usually teachable. It is more difficult to deal with those who arrogantly believe they have nothing more to learn or, more commonly, are so insecure they can't face their limitations and need for learning. In lonely isolation they often hunker down in self-defensiveness and stubbornly go on as they are. When dealing with such pastors I often wonder if this is sometimes true of me. I hope and pray that each of us becomes so secure in the grace of God and the compassion of our people that we will have courage to face our limitations honestly and to respond to them wisely.

LEARNING FOR COMPETENCE IN MINISTRY

Lifelong learning has much to do with stewardship of time, personal renewal, and habits of devotional life. Those concerns are the focus of chapters 6 and 10. In the rest of this chapter, we center on learning for competence in ministry.

Learning from People

Instead of lamenting our lack of time and money to read books and take continuing education courses, we begin with a source of learning available to every pastor with attentiveness to receive it: learning from people whose lives touch ours. Without taking time off from work or paying a nickel to anyone else, we can all follow the example of E. Stanley Jones, who said, "I try to learn something from every person I meet." I strongly affirm the importance of reading books and taking classes, but I also know that if we are open to learn from people, we will receive continual education.

While thankful for the many learned professors who have been my teachers, I am no less grateful for learning received from the ordinary folks with whom I grew up and the many similar people who have been my teachers in the parish. I think, for example, of a long conversation with an auto mechanic who told me of having killed several people during World War II: "I don't regret killing them," he said, "but, I deeply regret having had to do it." The discussion following his confession was as profound a learning experience for me, and perhaps also for him, as any in a seminary classroom.

I remember a woman who confessed after learning that her mother had terminal cancer, "I can't believe in God anymore!" During our visits we pondered the agonizing problem of human suffering, not just as a topic in a theological textbook but as a reality in experience. Through our visits, both of us, I believe, came to clearer understanding and renewed trust. A man told me of help he received when, as a teenager, he shared his doubts with a pastor and instead of being criticized was told, "Believe what you can!" That word of grace had blessed his life, and by sharing it he blessed mine.

I have learned much from people recovering with the help of Alcoholics Anonymous and Emotions Anonymous who have told their stories of lives broken, healed, and restored. Though often lacking in theological sophistication, they have helped teach me what it is to live by the grace of God.

Then there is the learning received from children and from students in confirmation classes. One student, Donna, couldn't remember Luther's answer to the question, "What does baptism mean for daily living?" But she taught me something when she answered, "It means that I can never be unbaptized." Bruce, who became a conscientious objector during the Vietnam War, taught me that indifference, and not hate, is often the opposite of love when he wrote in a confirmation essay, "War is a way nations have of settling their indifferences!"

Author Warren Bennis reports that "Ralph Waldo Emerson, one of our greatest American philosophers, used to greet old friends and acquaintances whom he hadn't seen for a while with the salutation, 'What's become clear to you since last we met?'"[2] That's a challenging question we wouldn't ask just anyone, but we might try it on some of our thoughtful friends. Instead of talking only about the weather and the last ball game, let's dare to ask about how things are with people. What is clear? What is confusing? What are their concerns and convictions? One old saint reported, "The older I become the fewer certainties I require." What an opening for vital conversation! What had become uncertain? What were the certainties now required? During and following such conversation we are compelled to ask ourselves, "Am I open to unlearn some things that I can no longer believe?" "Have I learned to live with fewer certainties?" and "What are the certainties that sustain my life?"

We are privileged to share our parishioners' joy and anguish. If we learn nothing from such experiences, the problem is ours. The parish is a great school, and every person we meet is a universe of mystery as vast and marvelous in its awesome complexity as the physical universe. Wisdom awaits us when we seek to learn something from every person we meet.

Beyond such general learning from people, I encourage all clergy to seek the companionship of an older and wiser pastor who can serve as a mentor. It has been said that when some people die, it's "like a library burning down." We need to find such people and ask what they have learned in their years of ministry. They may tell of habits we will not want to emulate or give advice we won't want to follow, but that too can be part of our learning. If they have any wisdom and we are smart enough to listen and learn, we will receive insights and suggestions that will enrich our lives and ministries.

Learning from Books

Book learning is another way of learning from people. When I wander through a library or bookstore, I often think of all the people I could meet and from whom I could learn if I had time to ponder what they have put on all those pages.

Among the most significant for our life and ministry are the people we meet in the books of the Bible. Without being legalistic about it, my habit for years has been to spend a half-hour reading the Bible early in the morning. Because I am usually preoccupied with final sermon preparation on Saturday and Sunday mornings, I usually don't do general Bible reading on those days. Early morning meetings, which I try to avoid, sometimes keep me from it, but these half-hours of biblical study and reflection usually happen four or five days a week. I recommend the habit to you. Some prefer to read a certain number of chapters or pages rather than for a period of time, but I find the latter more liberating. I am free, for example, to spend time checking cross references and parallel passages without feeling guilty for having failed to complete my "morning assignment." I also like to read one book at a time, rather than bits and pieces of several books, alternating between the New Testament and Old Testament with Apocrypha.

Even if you are skilled in biblical languages, I encourage you to also read an annotated English version. It will keep you from failing "to see the woods for the trees." Don't rush. Study the introduction to each book and read every footnote. Check out significant cross references. Read with a pencil: underline, and make notations in the margins. The Bible is to be chewed and digested, not just revered!

Reading the Bible and other significant works of theology slowly and carefully is lesson I learned from Professor Edmund Smits years ago. I had just completed a course in "efficient reading" and proudly told Dr. Smits of having received my "one thousand words per minute card" in recognition of that magnificent achievement. Instead of the expected word of congratulation, Smits responded as if in horror: "No! No! No!" he said. "You must read slowly! Great thinkers have poured their wisdom onto those pages, and you must carefully ponder every sentence." That advice doesn't fit everything we read. A thousand words per minute is too slow for some things that aren't worth reading, but it is much too fast for anything of substance and significance.

I must also confess that I do not find Bible reading to be consistently edifying and uplifting. I believe we err when we give that impression to our people. This sets them up for disappointment and probably helps account for the fact that many of those who sincerely resolve to read the Bible get bogged down and give up.

We need to be honest in recognizing that the Bible is not easy to read. It is a collection of diverse documents written in various literary forms over hundreds of years by many human authors. As Christians we believe that the Bible is God's Word to us. Paul Scherer put it well when he said, "God did not stop speaking when his book went to press."[3] But understanding what God has to say to us today in a particular text is not simple for either lay readers or clergy.

To those who argue for textual inerrancy, I propose that each of us spend a half-hour a day for one year reading an annotated version (such as the New Oxford or Harper Collins) with careful attention to footnotes and cross references. Then, let's get together again for frank and honest discussion of the biblical text.

Instead of struggling to maintain theories of verbal inspiration and textual inerrancy, it is far better, in my opinion, to honestly acknowledge biblical diversity and then to read all of scripture under the Lordship of Jesus Christ. We then see the written word in light of the Living Word who dwelt among us in the person of Jesus. If Jesus is Lord of all, he is also Lord of the Bible. If Jesus is not Lord of the Bible, I don't think he is Lord of anything!

Centered in Christ, we are free to let the Bible speak to us in all its diversity without fear that inconsistencies or contradictions will undermine our faith. As Christ-centered Christians, we do not believe in Jesus because of a theory of biblical inspiration. It is because of Jesus and the gospel message that centers in Christ that we eagerly turn to read the Bible as the source of God's Good News of life and salvation. Then the books come alive! We meet real people from different times and places with diverse and sometimes contradictory opinions. Assured by the central revelation of God's love and will in Jesus, we are freed from having to harmonize and homogenize everything in the Bible. Then we can deal honestly with all of Scripture, understanding every text in the context of Christ.

Other Theological Reading

I have often returned from theological conferences feeling guilty over books I have not read and overwhelmed by long lists of books I should be reading. After having served on a seminary faculty as well as in the parish, I confess displeasure with some professors who criticize pastors for having failed to read all the latest theological works they have so carefully studied. That's their job and they are given time to do it. Pastors have many other responsibilities and limited time for general theological study. Therefore, the question for us is, How do we best utilize our study time? What should we read?

Whatever you read, remember that "all truth is God's truth." When understood correctly, the truth we know in Jesus is not in conflict with realities revealed, for example, by historic and scientific research. Centered and grounded in Christ, we dialogue with those whose beliefs differ from our own (including adherents of other religions) in confidence that we have something significant to share and with openness to learn something new.

Rather than trying to read a little of everything and not much of anything, I recommend focused, selective reading and affirm Paul Scherer's suggestion that we should always be reading something we couldn't have written ourselves, both in terms of its difficulty a nd its perspective. You might, for example, select a specific author, such as Walter Brueggemann, Douglas John Hall, or Walter Wink, and then spend the next year reading all you can of what they have written.

Because Christian life centers in Jesus, I encourage you to study Jesus and to have the courage to read authors with whom you may disagree. I have been challenged by Marcus Borg's books on Jesus— *Jesus a New Vision, Meeting Jesus Again for the First Time,* and *Jesus in Contemporary Scholarship*—which raised many questions but also convinced me that we must deal seriously and honestly with the issues with which he wrestles. Whomever you study, remember this wisdom from the apostle Paul:

> For when one says, "I belong to Paul," and another, "I belong to Apollos," are you not merely human? What then is Apollos? What is Paul? Servants through whom you came to believe as the Lord assigned to each. . . . So let no one boast about human leaders. For all things are yours, whether Paul or Apollos or Cephas . . . all belong to you, and you belong to Christ, and Christ belongs to God (1 Corinthians 3:4-5, 21-23).

Paul reminds us that we do not belong to our teachers and are not slaves to anyone's thinking. All of our teachers belong to us and their wisdom is God's gift to us. Paul's perspective frees us from idolatrous attachment to any person or theological school of thought and opens us to learn from all.

I also encourage focused study of specific areas of ministry. I have sometimes spent a year or more trying to learn all I could about preaching, marriage and marriage counseling, grief and bereavement, Christian morality and the Ten Commandments, and the complex and controversial issues of life and death, (such as abortion, war, mercy killing, and the death penalty). I believe that these concentrated periods of study helped to enliven and enrich my ministry; they also resulted in my writing several little books on these subjects.

Some pastors find excitement and renewal by moving frequently from congregation to congregation. Such mobility, however, is not always possible or wise. Clergy in long-term ministries need not bog down and burn out. With determination we can bring new zest into our lives by focusing on areas of special interest. If we are well-bonded with our people and attentive to their needs, most congregations will affirm our spending 10 to 15 percent of our working time in such focused study. I encourage all of our congregations to provide their pastors with at least two weeks of study time annually (which can be accumulated to up to six weeks), with a modest stipend for education expenses. This is in addition to four weeks vacation. If your congregation makes such provision, use it—don't lose it, and don't waste it! If your congregation does not provide it, ask for it, not as a beggar, but because you are eager to improve your ministry.

Beyond that, we should remind our people that the Alban Institute recommends a three months sabbatical every four years. When we request such a sabbatical, we should present a study project indicating that were not just taking a prolonged vacation. If possible, use some sabbatical time to visit a Third World country to learn and to serve. Such encounters are often life transforming and ministry enriching.

Learning from Writing

Walter Bennis believes that "Writing is the most profound way of codifying your thoughts, and the best way of learning from yourself who you are and what you believe." He quotes William Faulkner, who said, "I don't know what I think until I read what I said."[4]

Learn what you think by putting your thoughts in writing. Your times of focused study may result in some thoughtful essays for your church newsletter. Whether you write for publication or not, I encourage you to keep a journal. I wish I had done so throughout my ministry, but I was always intimated by what seemed a laborious and time-consuming task. I was cured of that thinking by reading Ronald Klug's book *How to Keep a Spiritual Journal.* [5] With gracious winsomeness, Klug persuaded me to buy a notebook and start journaling. Sometimes my daily entry is only a brief summary of memories of the day. Other times it's a longer record of reflections and concerns that help me know what I am thinking. I recommend the habit to you.

Group Learning

My wife, Carol, and I have been members of a book discussion group for more than twenty years. All of the members of our group are clergy and clergy spouses, but to keep the clergy from talking shop and dominating the conversation, we never read anything explicitly theological. We meet monthly during the school year and usually discuss a novel or book of general interest. All of us have confessed that if it weren't for the group we wouldn't have read most of these books.

Carol and I are also part of a small mutual support group that combines social sharing with discussion of issues of personal concern. In addition to enjoying each other's company, we always ask how things are going for each of us and seek to provide care and encouragement for one another. If you are not a part of such a group, I would encourage you to join one—or perhaps even better, start one yourself. Coming into an established group is sometimes more difficult than starting from scratch. Many pastors tell of help received from groups that meet for discussion of the lectionary texts for the upcoming Sunday. While serving as a parish pastor, I was involved in such a group for a time and found the discussion insightful and an aid in sermon preparation. Some members did their homework and were the givers while others were largely receivers. If you are a member of such a group, commit yourself to be a contributor and not just a receiver.

I also encourage you to get involved with Alcoholics Anonymous, Alanon, Emotions Anonymous, and other Twelve Step programs.

Most have open meetings, and if your experience is like mine, you will seldom regret having attended.

Short-Course Learning

Attend short courses in areas of special interest to you or do disciplined study under the guidance of a seminary professor or mentor. Without retracting my encouragement to pursue areas of study that captivate us, I must warn against always doing what we like and neglecting what we need. If we need to improve our human relationship skills, we shouldn't use all our study time reading philosophical theology, even though that may be our delight. If all our recent study leave has involved church-growth seminars that we really enjoy, it may be time to take a course in biblical interpretation or systematic theology that we really need. We should be brave enough to invite some wise and trusted members to tell us what they think we need. It is certainly good to pursue study that enhances our strengths, but it is sometimes more important to focus on correcting some of our weaknesses.

Modern technology can facilitate learning. If we spend much of our time driving, a cassette player in the car becomes a necessity not a luxury, enabling us to feast on the abundant resources available on audiotapes. Videotapes of theological lectures and discussions are also increasingly available and can provide an excellent alternative to time wasted watching trivia on television. Computer networks may also be helpful, but beware of letting the fun of playing with computer technology distract you from more significant learning.

We who continually give must continually receive. Generosity without receptivity results in vacuity that has nothing to give. God has promised that "as your days, so shall your strength be," (Deuteronomy 33:25 RSV) and has assured us of grace sufficient to strengthen and sustain us in our weakness and limitations. God has also given us minds to learn and surrounded us with many opportunities for learning. Someone has said that "God gave each of us two ears and one mouth and we should take the hint." That suggests that we should spend twice as much time listening and learning as we do talking and teaching. As pastors we are blessed with the privilege and responsibility of being lifelong learners. Such learning is another of the vital habits that enable effective, lifelong, life-giving ministry.

5

Life-Giving Pastors
Have Something to Say and Say It Well

"So faith comes from what is heard, and what is heard comes from the preaching of Christ" (Romans 10:17 RSV).

I have done and have heard a lot of preaching. During ten years in my first parish, I preached almost every week. I was then called to teach homiletics at Luther Seminary and spent five years listening to sermons. There were ten more years of parish preaching followed by a dozen years as bishop that involved much preaching and many conversations with pastors and lay persons concerning preaching.

These experiences have taught me some things I would like to share in the hope that they will be helpful to your preaching. We will consider three basic questions and conclude with suggestions concerning how we can learn from our listeners. The questions are: 1) What is the purpose of preaching? 2) What do we have to say? and 3) How do we say it well?

WHAT IS THE PURPOSE OF PREACHING?

The purpose of preaching is identical to that of parish ministry: to give new life in Christ. The central theme for this book is also the theme for this chapter: "Go and stand in the temple and speak to the people all the words of this Life" (Acts 5:20 RSV). By quoting the Revised Standard Version (RSV), I emphasize the fact that it is "Life" with a capital L! This verse witnesses to the "Life . . . in all its fullness" (John 10:10 NEB) that Christ came to give.

In our preaching, we share the gospel message with the expectation that the Holy Spirit will use it to create new life in our listeners. We aren't just lecturers talking about the gospel or teachers explaining the life Christ comes to give, although we do such explaining and teaching in our preaching. In our proclamation, as in all our ministry, we are givers of new life in Christ. We are like one who gives drink to the thirsty and food to the hungry, like one who turns on the light in a room where people are stumbling in the dark. That drink and food and light are the life-giving gospel of God's grace in Jesus Christ. It is our opportunity, privilege, and responsibility to share God's grace in our preaching.

Some evangelists preach with urgency from the conviction that unless their listeners are saved by this sermon, they will spend eternity in hell. For pastors with a different theological perspective, that intense clarity of purpose is often lost. But aren't lots of people now living in the hell of meaningless and empty life? Isn't it a matter of tremendous importance and urgency that these people hear a message that can lift them to "walk in newness of life" (Romans 6:4)? Don't those of us who have heard this message and who have begun to walk this walk need to hear it again and again? Each of us needs repeated reassurance of grace that gives new life.

If we sometimes have doubts about the purpose of our preaching, we should ponder again the pastor's great commission: "Go and stand in the temple and speak to the people all the words of this Life" (Acts 5:20 RSV).

WHAT DO WE HAVE TO SAY?

Having affirmed such a vital purpose, we go on to ask, "What do we have to say that can create such life?" In reply, we thank God that in Jesus Christ we have glimpsed grace that gives life.

God Is on the Side of Life

The God we know in Jesus is on the side of life. John's gospel begins by saying of Jesus, "In him was life, and the life was the light of all people" (John 1:4). It ends by confessing that the whole book was written "that through believing you may have life in his name" (John 20:31).

Jesus taught that "those who want to save their life will lose it, and those who lose their life for my sake will save it" (Luke 9:24). That is not commandment; it is a fact of life. It's not true because Jesus said it; Jesus said it because it's true!

Witnesses to Jesus said that he taught with "authority" (Matthew 7:29). One way to translate that word is to say that Jesus spoke "out of the nature of things." Jesus revealed that this is for real: there are essentially only two ways to live. One is self-saving—the way of self-centeredness, self-indulgence, self-righteousness, self-preoccupation, and greedy, graspy selfishness. Those who live that way, said Jesus, lose the meaning of life. They are dying while they live and are as fruitless as a grain of wheat in the bin.

When caught up in that life, we may find temporary enjoyment in what the New Testament calls "the fleeting pleasures of sin" (Hebrews 11:25). But sooner or later we discover that there is something wrong with us on the inside. When we are quiet and honest with ourselves, it is as if we can hear a voice from within saying, "This is not it; this is not the life you are designed to live; this is not the person you were born to be."

When confronted with the futility of the self-saving life, we thank God that Jesus went on to say, "Those who lose their life for my sake will save it" (Luke 9:24). With those words, a new way of life opens before us. Jesus invites us to give ourselves away in trust of God and love of people. Then we may hear, perhaps as if for the first time, Jesus' words of invitation: "Come to me, all you that are weary and are carrying heavy burdens, and I will give you rest" (Matthew 11:28). And again, "Set your troubled hearts at rest. Trust in God always, trust also in me" (John 14:1 NEB).

As the love of God in Christ lures us out of self-saving living into the new adventure of self-losing living, we begin to give ourselves in surrender and abandonment to trust in God and to care for others. We let go of the idols to which we cling and rest our lives in God's mercy. We open the shuttered windows of life to welcome God's Spirit. Self-centeredness gives way to self-surrender. Selfishness and self-preoccupation give way to self-giving. To our amazement we discover that the kind of "self-losing" that Jesus invites and enables is not self-denying or self-degrading but self-fulfilling. Now if we listen to the song of our souls we hear a voice saying, "This is more like it. This has the touch and taste and feel of life in fullness. This is experiencing something of the life I was designed to live. This is being something of the person I was born to be."

When this happens and gratitude wells up within us, we know that it is all of grace—grace of mercy that welcomes and receives us, and grace of power that heals, lifts and enables us to walk in newness of life.

Then, as preachers, we know that there is a great gospel that bids us to proclaim it. My former colleague at Luther Seminary, John Hilbert, often said, "There are two kinds of preachers, those who have to say something and those who have something to say." In Christ we have something to say that is worth saying. It is the great "Yes" of the gospel. With the apostle Paul we say, "As surely as God is faithful, our word to you has not been 'Yes and No.' For the Son of God, Jesus Christ, whom we proclaimed among you . . . was not 'Yes and No' but in Him it is always 'Yes.' For in Him everyone of God's promises is a 'Yes'" (2 Corinthians 1:18-20). That life-giving "Yes" of God's grace is the heart and center of our message. Whatever the text of scripture from which we are preaching, the context is Christ and the gospel. Therefore we heed the wisdom of theologian C. F. W. Walther who reminded preachers long ago that we are not just to exhort people to have faith but are to "preach faith into their hearts by laying the gospel promises before them." [1]

Anti Anti-Life

If God is on the side of life, God must be against everything that denies, degrades, and destroys life. Sin is anti-life. Sin is not just against rules in a book, it is against life. Sin is sand in the gears of life. Sin undercuts life and empties it of joy and meaning. Grace enables, ennobles and fulfills life.

Our central affirmation of grace that gives life is rightly accompanied by a clear word of judgment over against all that is anti-life. It follows as night follows day that we who affirm life (and trust and thank God who gives and blesses life) cannot be indifferent to anything that diminishes life. We who love our children are rightly outraged when they are harmed or abused. The intensity of our distress and rage will, in fact, be in direct proportion to our love. Similarly, righteous rage has a place in our preaching. What saves it from being self-righteous is awareness that we, too, are sinners and stand under the same judgment, as well as the same mercy, that we proclaim to others.

Jesus said "Yes" to the self-losing life and "No" to the self-saving life. That "No" as well as that "Yes" should be part of our preaching. Having begun a pilgrimage of living by grace we stand against the "disgrace" of all sinful living. The proverb speaks the truth: "There is a way that seems right to a person, but its end is the way to death" (Proverbs 14:12). As we affirm the way of life, we stand against the ways of death. At its best our preaching is not sentimental sweet talk but a vital witness to the strong stuff of sturdy, life-giving grace and the ultimate futility and emptiness of graceless living.

Let's Get Going

Having said "Yes" to life and "No" to anti-life we still have something more to say, and that is the "Go" of those great commissions. I have called Acts 5:20 "The Pastor's and Preacher's Great Commission," but we have no monopoly on it. That verse, together with the other great commissions, is addressed to every Christian. We are all to be witnesses to and bearers of new life in Christ.

When speaking for Christ we not only say, "Come to me and I will give you rest," we also say, "Go for me and get to work." Like an ocean liner that both rests and works, we too (while resting in God's love) work—not to save ourselves but to save and bless the lives of others. An essential part of our preaching is the specific and concrete proclamation of the great commissions.

If we wonder if it is proper to proclaim the gospel to people of other religions, we should remember that the gospel is for all human beings and that we are called to be evangelists, not proselytizers. Proselytizers say, "My religion is better than your religion." Evangelists say, "God loves you, entrust your life to that love." We will never meet a person whom God doesn't love and to whom we can't make that statement and give that invitation. A missionary in India was asked, "How do you preach the gospel to a Hindu?" To which he replied, "I don't, I preach the gospel to a human being." That is an inadequate answer to a complex question, but it witnesses to a profound truth:

The gospel is for everyone! Our primary concern as evangelists is to proclaim to everyone we can, in every respectful way we can, the Good News of God's love in Jesus that invites, evokes and enables newness of life. In response to that life we of course will invite people to join a Christ-centered community, but increasing congregational membership should never be our basic goal.

HOW DO WE SAY IT WELL?

Having something to say, how best can we say it? Before trying to answer that question, it may be helpful for you to know what has created my present convictions.

At seminary, we were required to write manuscripts that were submitted to the professor before we preached them in class. When I returned to teach homiletics a decade later, that was still the practice, and as an obedient young professor I continued it in my classes. Before long, however, I grew tired of hearing students reading their sermons or attempting to recite them from memory.

Sermons were videotaped so the students could see and hear themselves, and I soon began the practice of having each of them answer a few questions following their sermons. We kept the camera running and were able to compare the way students spoke during their sermons and during the post-sermon responses. I was frequently struck by the fact that some of them really didn't talk to us until during that "P.S." They "gave their sermons" but didn't connect with their listeners.

I knew that something was wrong with this kind of preaching and at first blamed it on poor eye contact and lack of skill in reading. It was not until I read James McCroskey's *An Introduction to Rhetorical Communication* that I became aware of the real problem.[2] McCroskey taught me something that now seems as obvious as it is important, but which I had failed to recognize: *Vital communication happens when the person speaking is thinking the thoughts at the moment of utterance.*

Dull, lifeless communication happens when the speaker is reading or reciting words without thinking the thoughts as they are expressed. This, I then realized, was what was happening in much of the preaching I was hearing. In addition to their lifeless presentation, many of the sermons were confusing and disorganized. It was as if the students had ad-libbed at the typewriter. I had been given a manuscript but, as pastor Alvin Rueter liked to say of such a sermon, "There is nothing holding it together but the paper on which it is written!" It was only a stream of consciousness without evidence of careful selection and ordering of thought. No wonder the students had to read or recite it from memory. Without a clear plan of development there was no other way to do it.

In an attempt to correct both lifeless presentation and stream of consciousness development, I decided to abandon seminary tradition and change the assignment. The students were asked to stop writing manuscripts and instead to prepare a detailed plan that enabled us to see the sermon development. When it was well done, we could see how the sermon was to be introduced, the main points of its development, and the way in which it was to be concluded. Significant sentences could be written out, but the plan was to be sufficiently sketchy so that it could not be read. After developing this detailed plan, which could be several pages long, the students were to prepare a set of "as brief as possible" but "as long as necessary" sermon notes from which to preach. In essence they were asked to do two things: 1) in preparation, to carefully select and order their thought, and 2) in presentation, to think of their thought, and not just their words, at the moment of utterance.

I encouraged the students to think in terms of "chunks of thought" before thinking in terms of words and phrases. I affirm Linda Flower's advice for writers which, I believe, speaks even more to us preachers: "Don't write polished prose. . . . Don't stop to perfect spelling, grammar or even phrasing. Keep working at the level of ideas. . . . Try to keep your eye on the question or problem you have set for yourself."[3] In that statement I would underscore the importance of working at the level of ideas and for preachers would restate the ending: "Keep your eye on the text and theme you have set for yourself."

The several-page plan was really a detailed outline. But because some students had an aversion to "outlining," it seemed better to encourage the creation of a plan and to have them think of it as similar to what an architect does in designing a home. The several-page plan was to ensure that the sermon thought had been worked out in specific, concrete detail and that there were no gaps to be filled in by ad-libbing. The pulpit notes were to rekindle those thoughts in the mind of the preacher so that they were being relived during the preaching. The notes were to help the preacher share a carefully prepared message without reading or reciting words and sentences.

There was a lot of writing involved in the preparation of the detailed plan, but the students were reminded that they were preparing to speak, not to read what they had written. If they had created a sentence that was so precious it had to be said exactly as written, I encouraged them to write it into their pulpit notes and repeat it at least twice! At the same time, I reminded them that every sentence was not that precious and that they should risk having some awkward expressions or even forgetting something, but they should not risk becoming the kind of reading/reciting preachers who never communicate vitally and personally with their listeners.

THE PREPARATION PROCESS

We often discussed the distinction between "preparation *for* the sermon" and "preparation *of* the sermon." I advocate textual/thematic preaching. The preparation for such sermons centers on study of the text, commentaries, and other material related to the theme. Beyond that specific preparation, all of our lifelong learning and experience is an essential part of preparation for every sermon. The specific time of preparation *for* the sermon is what I call "the jotting stage" of sermon development, during which we jot down every significant insight and idea that comes to mind without attempting to order anything.

After having accumulated several pages of disordered jottings we turn to "preparation *of* the sermon," which essentially involves the selection and ordering of thought. Each sermon should focus on one central theme or unifying idea. When asked, "How many points should there be in a sermon?" I usually answer, "At least one." That one, however, is usually most clearly expressed when looked at from several angles that are clearly visible in the mind of the preacher, and then in the minds of the listeners, as the sermon progresses.

Someone has said that the three most important rules for preaching are 1) Be clear, 2) Be clear, and 3) Be clear. I'd say that the three most important rules are 1) Preach the gospel, 2) Be clear, and 3) Speak directly and personally to your listeners. But I realize that if we are not clear, it is unlikely that the gospel will be heard or our communication well-received.

I always begin the preparation of every sermon, or public talk of any kind, by writing the words, Introduction, Development and Conclusion, on a sheet of paper. I then draw a line down the right side of the page to create a margin so the page looks like this:

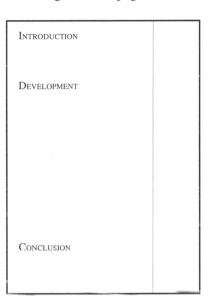

Then I begin thinking in terms of how I am going to introduce, develop, and conclude the sermon. I review my jottings and, again without attempting to order them, make note of the most promising ideas and illustrations in the right-hand margin. Then I rough out the first draft of a tentative plan of introduction, development, and conclusion. After reviewing it, I may decide to develop it further, or I may reject it and sketch out a different plan. After having prepared one or several one-page preliminary plans early in the week, I often put them aside to be developed further on following days. Even at this early stage I usually sense that I have a message that is worth sharing and, instead of being fearful of having to preach next Sunday, I look forward to the creative process of trying to figure out how best to share the message.

As I settle into a plan of development and work it out in specific detail, I attend to how it will be expressed. Some sections are almost written out, while others, such as stories and illustrations, are more briefly noted. Although it has been years since I practiced sermons out loud, I still go over them in my head and have specific patterns of expression in mind so that when I preach a sermon two or three times on Sunday morning it is nearly the same—but neither read nor recited.

Because printed words tend to get set and are resistant to change, Paul Scherer encouraged preachers to write with a pencil from beginning to end of sermon preparation and, even in this computer age, I still do so. A word processor enables easy revision and is well-suited to the preparation process I have described, but beware of ad-libbing at your computer and of thinking that your sermon is prepared when you have processed enough words to fill the sermon time. Whether we work with a 20-cent pencil or a $2,000 computer, no sermon is ever well-prepared without the careful selection and ordering of thought. This is true of narrative as well as expository sermons. Narrative sermons, too, need a clear beginning and ending and have stages or scenes of development—often more subtly expressed but no less real, than the chunks of thought in thematic/textual sermons.

Think and Tell

I once asked a popular senior pastor who did a lot of speaking to civic organizations and in other congregations, "How do you find time to prepare all those speeches?" "Well," he replied, "after a while you just open your mouth and listen to yourself talk."

I agree with Gerhard E. Frost that, "When asked to speak on short notice, we shouldn't always decline because of lack of time to prepare, but sometimes, at least, should be able to say, "I've been preparing for this all my life!"" But such speaking without preparation should happen only in emergency situations. The model I try to follow is not the pastor who listened to himself talk. I try to follow the example of Harry Emerson Fosdick, the first senior minister at Riverside Church in New York and the author of the great hymn "God of Grace and God of Glory." Fosdick said he never spoke in public without first attempting to "carefully order my thought." Clear preaching starts with clear thinking. Writers Herbert and Jill Meyer have good counsel for speakers as well:

> The absolute first thing to do when you launch a writing project is to resist the impulse to start writing. You need to relax, to settle down, and above all you need to think. Don't worry about wasting time; it's never a waste of time to get your thoughts in order.[4]

Thinking that results in careful ordering takes time and is hard work, but it is also challenging, exciting, and essential to good preaching.

Someone has said, "Success is often only an idea away!" I believe that to be true of our preaching. The process of moving from text and theme to sermon is a creative adventure, like designing a house, or creating a useful new product. This doesn't mean that our sermons are merely demonstrations of cerebral brilliance, void of feeling and emotion. I encourage the use of stories, illustrations, and examples that move us at the deepest level of our emotional and spiritual life. But at the same time I have learned in my experience as a listener that clear thought and sincere emotion go best together.

Some teachers of homiletics, such as Alvin Reuter (whose book *Making Good Preaching Better* I recommend to you) advocate preaching without notes.[5] When our sermons are clearly ordered, we should be able to preach without looking at notes, but I still like to have a sketch of the sermon plan with me in the pulpit. I seldom look at the notes, but they save me from being preoccupied with remembering; they enable me to focus on my message and my listeners. I may write out a few choice sentences, but even these are not just to be read. They, like the rest of the outline, are to rekindle my thoughts and enable me to think of my ideas while sharing them.

If preaching without a full manuscript in front of you seems scary, take a first step in the direction of more vital preaching by telling, instead of reading or reciting, all illustrations and stories from personal experience. Then take further steps by personally sharing the introduction, conclusion, and best-prepared portions of the sermon. I guarantee that your listeners will like it and that when you get used to it you will also enjoy more direct, personal preaching.

Risk Being "For Real"

Beware of anything and everything that keeps you from being yourself in the pulpit. There is something about pulpits and sermonizing that ruins a lot of good speakers. From my perspective some preachers' most vital, personal communication is during the announcements, not during the sermon. The announcements are earthy and real while the sermons are other-worldly and ethereal. Alvin Rogness suggested, "Preachers should talk about the gospel the way a farmer talks about a Holstein cow." If we are other than our natural selves when preaching, it may say more about our personal insecurities than our homiletical skills. E. Stanley Jones reported that he felt affirmed when someone said after a sermon, "You didn't preach at us. You just told us things." Don't try to preach great sermons. Simply and honestly tell what you have learned from Jesus and the Bible that is significant for you and your listeners.

There is no substitute for genuineness. Our thoughts, words, and attitudes reveal who we are in mind and heart and will be expressed in one way or another. People will come to know and respond to the persons we are and not to just the pastors and preachers, we intentionally or subconsciously pretend to be. If pretense is part of our preaching, we need compassionate confrontation and counsel or therapy to correct it.

Learn from Your Listeners

Preaching without listener response is like driving golf balls in the dark. No one but our listeners can tell us if our sermons are "hitting the green." To be the best preachers we can be, we need to hear from our listeners.

It is scary to invite sermon feedback. Someone has said that "when we open our mouths, we let people look into our hearts and minds." Sermon evaluation is also preacher evaluation, and because none of us is perfect, we may be threatened by such scrutiny. But we need to risk it. Whether our listeners tell us or not, they have impressions of our sermons and of us. Isn't it better that we know what they think and feel rather than living in ignorance? Most people are compassionate and kind, and their comments will be encouraging and their suggestions helpful.

I still remember two comments made by Herman Hagen, a hardware dealer in my first parish: "You look at the congregation," he said, "but when we sit in the front pew you never look us in the eye."

And, "Your preaching is zestful and enthusiastic, but you speak with such a steady, rapid pace that it is easy after a while to sit back and let the sermon go over our heads." I needed those comments and thereafter marked my sermon notes with reminders to look at the people in the front pew, to slow down, and sometimes to stop completely and break the steady pace of my preaching.

To learn from our listeners, I recommend having sermon feedback cards in the pew racks every Sunday. They might say:

Sermon Reactions? Preaching Suggestions?

To help make preaching a two-way street, please write your sermon reactions (positive and negative) and suggestions on this card and return it with the offering or hand to an usher. You need not sign your name. Thank you.

Or a little larger card or bulletin insert might say:

Partnership Preaching

You are invited to be a partner in the preaching process. Please share your sermon reactions and suggestions on this form. Return to the offering plate, hand to an usher, or mail to the church. You need not sign your name.

1. What did you appreciate in the sermon?

2. What detracted?

3. What should I do to improve my preaching?

In addition to asking for written feedback, I encourage you to invite six to eight kind and honest parishioners to meet with you once a month for six months to discuss your preaching. During the first session, ask them to share childhood memories of preaching and to tell of preaching they heard before meeting you. As an assignment for the second session, give them copies of the "Partnership in Preaching" form and tell them that, because you need encouragement, you would like them to spend the next session sharing everything they can think of that they appreciate and have found helpful in your preaching. During subsequent sessions, invite them to talk about what they have found distracting and encourage them to share their suggestions for improvement. Enforce the rule that while general affirmations are acceptable, general negative comments are forbidden. Remind them that you receive encouragement when they say, "Thanks for a good sermon," that it is worse than useless to be told "I didn't like that sermon." Negative comments are welcome, but they need to be specific. They must tell exactly what they don't like so that you will have something to react to and learn from. Also encourage them to express their negative comments in the form of positive suggestions for improvement and not just as complaints.[6]

As part of the feedback process, you might even invite the group to read this chapter and discuss it with you. After six months of feedback on your preaching, you may wish to have the same or another group meet with you for discussion of other aspects of your ministry. Selected sections or chapters of this book may provide the springboard for such conversation.

The call to preach life-giving sermons week after week is a great privilege and a great challenge. It is sustained by great promises that assure us that God's grace is sufficient for us and that God will never fail us or forsake us. We thank God that in Christ we have been given something exceedingly significant to say and we welcome every means of improving our ability to say it well.

In closing, I share this thought and recommendation from Paul Scherer: "The sermon should move the congregation to want to pray and the preacher should, therefore, lead them in a brief post-sermon prayer asking God to effect in our lives what the sermon has promised and proclaimed." I have followed Scherer's suggestion for nearly forty years and commend it to you.

6

Life-Giving Pastors
Are Good Stewards
of Time

"Be careful then how you live, not as unwise people but as wise, making the most of the time . . ." (Ephesians 5:15).

Time management is a problem for many pastors. I am glad to report that the most serious marital difficulties Carol and I have related to how I spend my time. I'm glad—not for those problems but for our having had no more serious difficulties in our life together. I'd give myself a B-minus on time management, but know there have been days when Carol would have given me a D-minus or perhaps an F!

During my ten years in my first parish, our children were young and Carol did not work outside the home. The parsonage was close to the church, and we usually had all our meals together. There were many evening meetings, and except for mealtimes Carol was alone with the children from morning until night. During the first years, I was a solo pastor with a part-time secretary. With responsibility for everything at that time, I was at least as busy as I was later as a senior pastor with a staff in a larger congregation. In retrospect, I think it was more difficult, especially in terms of time management, to be a solo than a senior pastor.

We made valiant efforts to preserve family time together. For example, there were about a dozen Bible study groups meeting monthly in homes of members. Most met at 7:30 P.M. If I had tried to attend them all, I would have missed a lot of bedtimes with our children. Instead of either refusing to attend the Bible studies or giving up that much precious family time, we agreed that the laity would be on their own for most of the meeting. By 8:30 or 9 P.M. when our children were asleep, we often had a sitter come so that Carol and I could attend the coffee hour conclusion of a Bible study during which I responded to issues and questions that had been raised by the group. This proved to be a win-win arrangement not only for me but for the laity who discovered that they could have meaningful Bible study without the presence, or intimidation and domination, of a pastor.

During my years as a seminary professor, Carol and I had few time-management problems. She was a part-time elementary school librarian, our children were in school, and our schedules meshed beautifully. Except for occasional preaching, my weekends were free, and we shared vacation times together. This doesn't mean that seminary teaching is easier than parish ministry, but it is certainly more conducive to harmonious time management.

When I became senior pastor of University Lutheran Church of Hope, we quickly discovered that our schedules were again badly out of sync. Carol was now a full-time librarian, and our children were in junior and senior high. Multiple worship services and frequent weddings occupied my weekends, and there were many evening meetings. We seemed to handle the adjustment quite well, and I commented to Carol on how few time-management problems we were having. Her response cleansed me of my pride and put the matter in more proper perspective: "The reason for that," she said, "is that we don't need you as much anymore!" That was not a sarcastic putdown; it was simply a fact of our life together. With Carol's library responsibilities and our children's involvement in school activities, when I had an evening at home they were often elsewhere!

This reminds me to encourage those of you with young children to be vigilant in guarding the treasure of family time. God's call to ministry is not a call to neglect our families. We have only one opportunity to be with our children during their childhood and with our spouses in early marriage. Pastors without spouses or children also have family and friends and need to take time to nourish these relationships. If we miss times of vital togetherness, we can never go back and live them again. As the melancholy poet reminds us:

> The Moving Finger writes; And, having writ,
> Moves on: Nor all your Piety nor Wit
> Shall lure it back to cancel half a Line,
> Nor all your Tears wash out a Word of it.[1]

Soon after my election as bishop of the Southeastern Minnesota District of the American Lutheran Church, I asked Herbert Chilstrom, then bishop of the Minnesota Synod of the Lutheran Church of America, what I should expect. He replied by telling me of a new bishop who asked a predecessor, "What do I do in this job?" To which the wise old bishop replied, "When you come into your office on the first day, your secretary will hand you a huge stack of paper—correspondence to be answered, materials to be carefully read and mastered—then the phone will ring, and you will never again ask, 'What do I do in this job?'" That's an exaggeration, but not by much. I have often said that we should have two bishops—a "people bishop" and a "paper bishop." Perhaps there should also be a "telephone bishop"! In this setting, too, I found time management difficult. But am grateful I never had time to get bored!

TWO PERSISTENT PROBLEMS FOR PASTORS

Two problems in time management are especially significant for pastors. They are not mutually exclusive and often coexist in our pastoral life. On the one hand, we personally manage our own time. We don't punch a clock, and there is no one telling us exactly what to do every hour of the day. On the other hand, expectations come at us from many directions, and many people are, in effect, trying to tell us what to do. We are, to paraphrase Martin Luther, "free lords subject to none," while at the same time "slaves of all, subject to many." Is it any wonder that we have problems with time management?

While attending seminary forty years ago, a beloved professor told us how to manage our time. Every morning was to be spent "in the study," doing sermon and Bible study preparation, theological reading, and reflection. (Note that he said "in the study" and not "in the office.") We might need to spend a little time in the early afternoon with correspondence and office detail but on most afternoons we were to be busy with hospital, shut-in, outreach, and general parish visitation. After dinner there would sometimes be church council and committee meetings, but we would usually be home with our families.

Perhaps that was typical of a pastor's life seventy years ago when that professor was serving a congregation, but it is not what I experienced.

Whenever I was doing anything, I was often aware of many other things I wasn't doing. There were days in the parish, and more as a bishop, when I felt like the person who mounted a horse and rode off in all directions! I think it is more difficult to be a pastor now than it was even a dozen years ago. The expectations for performance and program development in many places are immense, and the competition among congregations is intense and sometimes disturbing.

In this context how do we best manage our time? As a survivor of the struggle and with humility born of many failures, I offer some suggestions that I hope will be helpful:

Suggestion 1
Dare to trust that Paul Tournier was right when he said, "God has given each of us enough time to do what God wants us to do."

When I first read that years ago it was a great word of grace for me, and I hope it can also be for you. God has not given us enough time to do everything everybody wants us to do or even enough time to do everything we would like to do. But God has given us enough time to do what God wants us to do.

Time management for all Christians, including pastors, is steward-ship of God's time. It means beginning each day with thanks for time and ability sufficient to do what God wants us to do, and with a prayer of surrender asking for the wisdom to know what that is and the willingness to do it. When overwhelmed with responsibilities beyond our time and ability, remember the person who said, "The best day in my life was when I resigned from being chair of the board of the universe." Such daily resignation is good for all who are stewards of God's time.

Suggestion 2
Order your priorities.

Living in the assurance that there is sufficient time to do what God wants us to do is helpful, but it doesn't answer the next question: "What does God want me to do?" Because we have no direct line to God, the best we can do is to prayerfully order our priorities in light of the values and life purposes we see in Jesus. When Jesus affirmed his disciples' law-breaking and said, "The sabbath was made for humankind and not humankind for the sabbath" (Mark 2:27), he clearly declared that all people and all human institutions are given to serve human need and that people are not just to serve institutions. With Jesus people came first. His purpose in every circumstance was to act with life-giving love and he set things straight for his disciples when he said:

> You know that the rulers of the Gentiles lord it over them, and their great ones are tyrants over them. It will not be so among you; but whoever wishes to be great among you must be your servant, and whoever wishes to be first among you must be your slave; just as the Son of Man came not to be served but to serve, and to give his life as a ransom for many (Matthew 20:25-28).

Here is a clear standard for the ordering of priorities for all of Jesus' followers, and most certainly for those of us who have accepted his call to life-giving ministry.

As we wrestle with the ordering of our priorities, we continually ask ourselves questions such as: "Does what I am doing express the life-giving gospel of Christ?" "Do my activities advance the mission and ministry of Christ or am I primarily involved in the maintenance of an institution?" "Am I, with Jesus, putting people first?" "Are my chief concerns to give and to serve or to get and be served?"

Struggling with such questions doesn't tell us what to do every hour of the day, but it does provide a Christ-centered context for the ordering of our priorities and helps free us from both aimless drifting and letting others control our lives. Being surrendered to God, we surrender to no one else nor to our own lazy indecisiveness. As much as humanly possible, we are, under God, in control of our lives and times.

Suggestion 3
Distinguish between the urgent and the important.

Things that are urgent but not important often crowd out things that are important but not urgent. We pastors sometimes allow ourselves to be distracted by the detail of a hundred urgencies. Each has some minimal value, but even when added together they are not of great importance. Nevertheless, they fill our hours and days and keep us from the vital work we are called to do. Because they give us an excuse to put off significant and difficult things we don't like to do, we may even welcome such distractions. When so tempted, each of us should follow the example of E. Stanley Jones, who said that he did at least one thing every day that he didn't like to do.

But again we ask, "How do we know the urgent from the important? Aren't some things both urgent and important?" Of course. But many things that are urgent are not all that important. The ringing telephone is urgent, but its message may be important or it may only be trivial. Near the phone is a stack of books. I know that it is important for me to read them, but no one has given me a deadline for their completion. If reading them is important, shouldn't I set such a deadline for myself? When I do so, I elevate the reading of those books from the category of "things that are important but not urgent" into "things that are both important and urgent."

Many find it helpful to use an A, B, C system. Things that are urgent and important are class A priorities. Things that are important but not immediately urgent are in category B, and those that are neither urgent nor very important fall in category C. These are the maybes of life that may get done if there is time to do them. As time passes, we discover that some items move from one category to another. Some of those "A"s really aren't all that important. Some of the "B"s may become "A"s or "C"s and some "C"s may move up or be dropped altogether.

One of the keys to getting things done is to know what to leave undone. If we are ever to do anything, we can't do everything. One of the essential arts of parish ministry is the art of living with unfinished business, the art of leaving many things undone so that we can do the things that need to be done, the art of distinguishing between the vital and the trivial, the essential and the important, the best and the good.

Because we all have blind spots and make flawed judgments, it is often helpful to periodically review the ordering or our priorities with an objective mentor. As parish pastors, we should also discuss our priorities with respected lay leaders and, as much as possible, keep our personal goals in harmony with congregational priorities. It is much easier for us to say no to distracting temptations from within ourselves or from others when we can reply that "the church council and I agree that these are the priorities for ministry."

In my experience, most congregations and pastors agree that clear proclamation of the gospel, meaningful worship, being a welcoming community, caring for the hurting, teaching and guiding children and adults, inspiring responsible stewardship, and standing for justice for the oppressed are high priorities—but they often differ on the exact ordering. I think that's OK. We need diversity of emphasis among our congregations and pastors.

At the same time, we all need to beware of riding our own hobby-horses! I believe, for example, that preparation for preaching is a very high priority. But I would not affirm pastors who said they didn't have time for involvement in congregational activities because they were working on their sermons. Worship is certainly a high priority, but if we are in a situation of conflict and estrangement, something else may take precedence. Then we may need to heed these words of Jesus: "So when you are offering your gift at the altar, if you remember that your brother or sister has something against you, leave your gift before the altar and go; first be reconciled to your brother or sister and then, offer your gift" (Matthew 5:23-24). Jesus reminds us to beware of temptations to let anything of importance keep us from that which is absolutely essential, in this case reconciliation with a brother or sister. We need to be continually vigilant lest the good become the enemy of the best and the important a substitute for the essential.

Suggestion 4
Schedule to force prioritization.

At University Church of Hope, all twelve of the congregational commissions, as they were called, met at the same time, so it was impossible for each pastor to attend them all. That frustrated me at first, when I was trying to get acquainted with things and people, but I soon became thankful because it forced both me and the commissions to order priorities. I went to the commissions to which I was specifically invited and with which I had significant concerns, stopping briefly at others if I had time.

81

Suggestion 5
Plan ahead.

Jesus taught that we, like the birds of the air and lilies of the field, are to live with such basic trust in our heavenly Father that we don't worry even about the necessities of life. We are specifically told, "So do not worry about tomorrow, for tomorrow will bring worries of its own. Today's trouble is enough for today" (Matthew 6:34). On the other hand, Jesus affirmed the common sense of builders and kings who plan ahead (see Luke 14:28-32), and it seems likely that he would agree with those who have said that "Wisdom consists in the anticipation of consequences" and "Planning for tomorrow is today's work."

As an example of such planning, I have found it helpful and anxiety reducing to begin sermon preparation well in advance. I kept a loose-leaf notebook with several pages for each of the next month's Sundays, read the lectionary texts several weeks in advance and began jotting ideas that might turn up in those future sermons. I never attempted to fully prepare a sermon that early, but taking those first steps saved me from the panic of frantic, last-minute preparation. It also enabled me to practice the wisdom of former Luther Seminary president T. F. Gullixson, who taught us to "let your sermon texts and themes stew in the juices of your subconscious mind."

While encouraging us to take time for recreation on a regular day off, Paul Scherer also told us that we should never leave for golf on Monday morning without having read, hopefully not for the first time, the text for the following Sunday. The practice of planning ahead and mental "stewing" enabled me to do a some sermon preparation while shaving or driving my car. Wise pastors also lead their congregations in planning ahead. An annual planning retreat is often helpful as is monthly review of progress and difficulties related to the fulfillment of the congregation's goals and objectives. We all feel better and work better when we know where we are and where we are headed.

Suggestion 6
Confront personal time-management problems.

Dealing with paper. Each of us must deal with specific problems of time management. One of mine was in dealing with the paper that piled up on my desk. Even though I know the rules: Handle paper only once and respond to correspondence after first reading it so that you don't have to read twice. (When corresponding with someone who will immediately respond to each of your letters with a long letter of questions and complaints, it is sometimes wise to put off posting the letter.) But under the pressure of limited time, I often scanned the mail and put it aside to read and respond to later. My tendency to read whatever crosses my desk before tossing it in the recycle box also helped build piles of paper. When the stacks got embarrassingly high, even for me, I sometimes quoted Gerhard Frost, who said, "My messy office is a symbol of my messy life." I also shared lines from one of Frost's poems, "Saturday Morning":

> Lord, you know,
> I've been straightening my desk,
> and I needn't tell you
> I'm a piler, not a filer,
> and if I were a filer
> I'd still lose things—
> alphabetically, I mean.
>
> So, Lord, as you once brooded
> over primeval chaos,
> let your Spirit brood today
> over this clutter
> which is my life,
> lest I lose myself,
> and you
> the Eternal Best.[2]

I am also a piler in the sense of preferring to stack paper to be saved in the cubicles of small-drawer cabinets rather than putting it in file folders. It is easier for me to toss something in a drawer than to fuss around in file cabinets. One pastor has a whole wall of such cubby-holes, including one for each Sunday of the year and each session of confirmation class. He uses these in planning for preaching, teaching, special events, and for the ordered "piling" of things he wants to save.

Someone once told me, "Your job is to work yourself out of a job." One step in that direction is to follow the advice of publisher Malcolm Forbes, who said, "The way to handle paper is to hand it to someone with instructions on what to do with it." If we have limited staff support, that may not seem to be great advice. But before rejecting it, we should take another look at ourselves and the people around us. Do we get self-righteous satisfaction out of trying to do everything on our own? Is there a staff person or volunteer to whom we could hand some of that paper?

Philosopher Alfred North Whitehead had a way of dealing with correspondence that I can't recommend, but it does witness to his ordering of priorities. One of his graduate students reported that Whitehead once waved toward letters piled about him in his study and said with an apologetic smile, "Always answer your letters and keep your desk tidy. I don't answer mine because it interferes with my concentration on more pressing matters."[3] There may be times when concentration on more pressing matters keeps us from immediately responding to correspondence, but we should always remember that there are people behind that paper and respond by letter or phone as soon as possible.

Trying to do too much in too little time. Another of my besetting sins of time management is attempting to do too much in too little time. Before leaving for a meeting, for example, I often try to squeeze in one more telephone call, and if it is longer than expected, I'm late for the meeting. Someone has said that "when we're late, we are hostile; when we're early, we are anxious; when we're on time, we are compulsive"—so perhaps we can't win. But if we don't like to be kept waiting, we should not unnecessarily keep others waiting for us. Here again, we need to remember that if we are going to do anything, we've got to stop trying to do everything!

Managing meetings. During many long meetings I have thought of founding a support group called "Meetings Anonymous." The first step will be, "We admitted that we were powerless over meetings and that our lives had become unmanageable." We will follow the other eleven steps of A A but will have no meetings. On meeting night we will all stay home! We should often ask, "Is this meeting necessary?" Could a few phone calls or a brief conference call suffice? Because meetings keep us busy and give the appearance of work, we may be tempted to continue them even when they accomplish little. At the same time, meeting together can deepen bonding and strengthen personal relationships, and these factors should also be considered when evaluating their usefulness.

Time for individuals. One pastor told of having solved his time-management problem by declaring, "I am so busy that I no longer have time for individuals." It is, no doubt, possible to spend too much time with individuals, and, unless we are trained therapists, it is probably wise to limit our pastoral counseling to only a few sessions and to refer those who need more help to a long-term therapist. But if the time comes when we are too busy to see individuals, we are busier than Jesus and need help in reordering our priorities. Jesus was often on the move but seems never to have been in a hurry. Jesus sometimes went away from people to have times alone, but he didn't drive people away. Even when his disciples urged him to "send her away," Jesus had time for a troubled women (Matthew 15:21-28). This reminds me of a pastor who said, "I was distressed with interruptions that disturbed my work until I realized that interruptions are part of my work." Each of us should have a plan for the day but should also live the plan with graciousness, not legalistic rigidity. Willingness to modify the plan is less stressful for ourselves and contributes to health and harmony in both pastor and congregation.

Polyactivity. Because I sometimes try to do more than one thing at a time, such as signing letters while talking on the telephone, I have been accused of being *polyactive.* Although doing two things at once is often detrimental to both, as well as to our mental and emotional health, it is sometimes wise and beneficial. I like to read the morning paper and at least some of each of the many magazines to which we subscribe. I also affirm the importance of physical exercise but had difficulty finding time to do it. Then I got an exercise bicycle with a reading stand and by reading while I ride have in effect added 30 to 45 minutes to my day. After more than 15,000 biking-while-reading miles, I recommend it to you as healthy exercise and good stewardship of time.

Having confessed my struggles, I should also acknowledge that I've heard of clergy whose time-management problems are very different from mine. They have discovered that it's easy to be a parish pastor. They buy and preach other people's sermons and seem dedicated to minimal, maintenance ministry that involves as little work as possible. Anyone who cares enough to read this book is probably not among such clergy. If such are your habits, however, I think you need some help. What specifically is your problem? Are you simply lazy, or are you discouraged and depressed? Don't bear those burdens alone. (I am convinced that clinical depression is a physical illness with an excellent prognosis if properly treated.) Whatever your need, there is help for you in Christ and the Holy Spirit together with a good mentor, therapist, or medical doctor. If you are feeling burned out, may the grace of God and the help of people give you new hope and healing for life and ministry.

A CONCLUDING PARABLE

In *When the Last Acorn Is Found*, Deborah Latzke quotes the parable of the acorn people:

> Everyone age five to sixty-five wears a watch. But instead of marking time with minutes and hours, their time keepers merely flash a single iridescent word: now. Youngest and oldest acorns have no need to wear a watch, for they never seem to forget . . . now is what truly matters.[4]

"Now," said Paul Tillich, "is the moment when eternity touches time." Now, in this and every present moment, God graces our lives with mercy and power. Now we rejoice in the Lord, now we work and now we rest. Between the past that is no more and the future that is not yet, we live all life long in the time called "now." The ultimate test of our stewardship of time is not in what we did yesterday or will do tomorrow, but in what we are doing now. As we live in that now, venturing from the no more to the not yet, may our stewardship of that precious moment enable both life-fulfillment in us and life-giving ministry to others.

7

Life-Giving Pastors
Pick Their Battles Wisely
and Fight Them Fairly

"If it is possible, so far as it depends on you, live peaceably with all. . . . Let us then pursue what makes for peace and for mutual upbuilding" (Romans 12:18 and 14:19).

A young pastor once told me of tension between himself and some members of the congregation, and then said he'd like a parish "that doesn't have any of these problems with difficult people." I was sorry to have to confess that, although there may be such a congregation somewhere, I didn't know of any. The New Testament tells of problems in the first churches, and that's been the same story ever since.

An elderly pastor's widow told me that when her husband was serving his first parish, he wrote to his parents complaining about problem people in the congregation. In reply, they reminded him that he shouldn't complain because that was why he was there—to love and serve those people and to help them deal with their problems, including their difficulties in dealing with him.

While thankful for all of life's joys, we remember that we live in a troubled world and that we are called to serve churches with troublesome people who must sometimes deal with troublesome pastors. In ministry, as in the rest of life, tensions and conflict come with the territory.

Peace is not the absence of conflict but the non-violent management and resolution of conflict. If that is true of the world in general, what about peace in the church? Peace in the church is not the absence of conflict but the non-violent, civilized, and even Christian, management and resolution of conflict.

87

What then is the pastor's role in dealing with this conflict, especially with congregational conflict that often centers in the performance and person of the pastor? In the midst of conflict, how do we pick our battles wisely and fight them fairly?

I began wrestling with this question early in my first parish and it has been a frequent concern ever since, especially during my years as a bishop. I have no perfect answers, but lessons taught by the hard school of experience and learned from others have enabled me to see some things that I would like to share in the hope they will be helpful.

To set the stage, I will cite several examples of common congregational conflict and then suggest ways of continuing life-giving ministry in such situations. Conflicts related specifically to prophetic ministry will be considered in chapter 8.

EXAMPLES OF COMMON CONGREGATIONAL CONFLICT

Factions fighting over old grudges. You discover soon after beginning a new ministry that there are feuding factions in the congregation that no one had told you about. Old grudges have been carried for years. Some, for example, are still angry over how a pastor they liked was forced out twenty years ago. Or there may be a group that was resentful over the congregation's decision to follow through on plans for a new building a decade ago, and this group may now be convinced that they were right. There is superficial civility but underlying tension and hostility. You sense subtle pressure from people in each faction to take their side.

Withdrawal of support for the pastor's vision. The call committee and council welcomed you enthusiastically and affirmed the vision of ministry you shared with them. You were exactly the minister they were looking for, and the changes you proposed were just what they wanted. But now you begin to wonder. Did they really speak for the majority of this 75-year- old congregation? Even some of those who have been most affirming now seem to have second thoughts. Are they overreacting to complaints from others, or are they having a change in heart?

and even honest expression of anger, but not for hurtful sinning. We often let troublesome people "hook us" into excessive anxiety, and even into treating them as they are treating us. In stormy situations, we need to remember that all the water in the world can't sink a ship unless the water gets inside. When storms are raging, we pray for what Edwin Friedman called "capacity to maintain a (relatively) non-anxious presence [that] will modify anxiety throughout the entire congregation."[6] When tempted to be less than unconditionally constructive, we do well to ponder these words:

> So then, putting away all falsehood, let all of us speak the truth to our neighbors, for we are members of one another. Be angry but do not sin; do not let the sun go down on your anger, and do not make room for the devil. . . . Let no evil talk come out of your mouths, but only what is useful for building up, as there is need, so that your words may give grace to those who hear. . . . Put away from you all bitterness and wrath and anger and wrangling and slander, together with all malice, and be kind to one another, tenderhearted, forgiving one another, as God in Christ has forgiven you (Ephesians 4:25-27, 29, 31-32).

Suggestion 2
Maintain objectivity;
don't personalize every conflict.

We have responsibilities and should take them seriously. We make mistakes and should say, "I'm sorry." When in difficulty with a troublesome person, we should sometimes confess—not attack or criticize, but confess—"I'm having difficulty working with you and would like to visit about it." Or, "What can I do to make it easier for us to work together?" Even when we are convinced that we have done nothing wrong, we can say, "I'm sorry that what I said, or did, felt hurtful to you." In *A Handbook to Marriage*, Theodor Bovet observes that when each spouse is convinced of being 100 percent right and the other 100 percent wrong, there is deadlock, but when each of them admits to being two percent wrong and they "try to remedy the . . . two percent and apologize for it, the row is a hundred percent over."[7] The same is often true in the church. With our understanding of the universality of

Unelected, old-guard leaders. You wonder who is really running this church? There are some great people in positions of elected leadership, but there is a group of men who meet for coffee almost every morning. Their wives seem to be the real power in the women's group and maybe even in the congregation. Some of the elected lay leaders seem eager for change, while others seem fearful and intimidated, and they don't want to do anything without the blessing and support of the old guard.

Problems with inherited staff and lay workers. You are having trouble dealing with some of the staff and volunteer leaders who were on the scene when you arrived. The organist and secretary are both members who have served the church for more than fifteen years. Neither strikes you as especially gifted, and both seem cool to you and any new ideas. The volunteer Sunday school superintendent has had that job for twenty years, and three years ago persuaded the council to replace your denomination's education material with resources from an independent publisher that are so bad that you hate having to inflict them on your own, as well as other's, children.

Some people don't seem to like you. Although you have tried to be kind and courteous to everyone, you are beginning to wonder if there are some people who just don't like you and who really haven't accepted you as their pastor. Someone may even have been as frank with you as was one woman who told me, "There are six things my husband and I don't like about you," and then described them in detail.

Discord over building plans. You are thrilled with the life and growth of your congregation. Membership has increased by 25 percent since you arrived five years ago. The enthusiasm of your members together with a major housing development nearby seem to almost guarantee continued growth. You already have multiple worship services and church school sessions, and will soon outgrow your present building. Some members want to expand at the present location while others are enthusiastic about relocating to a site on the edge of town. Sentiment seems equally divided, and there are significant pros and cons on each side. Convictions are so intense that you fear that either decision will cause discord and division, and perhaps even split the congregation.

Conflict over styles of worship. After years of traditional worship, some members are beginning to complain. A nearby congregation of your denomination is attracting many people, including a few of your members, to its contemporary worship services. Some parishioners encourage you to follow that congregation's example while others have said, "Please don't start anything like that over here."

Complaints concerning ministry with youth. You are thrilled with your congregation's confirmation and youth program, and the kids seem to be having a great time. The attendance and the spirit of the group have never been higher. Now several members have come to complain: Why aren't there more Bible studies? Why isn't more memory work required? High schoolers were seen smoking outside the church, and there were rumors of a teenage beer party and that one of the girls had gotten pregnant and may have had an abortion. You are challenged to provide better supervision, stronger moral guidance, and a "more Christian" youth program.

HOW DOES A PASTOR MINISTER EFFECTIVELY IN SUCH SITUATIONS?

It's not easy! But there are better and worse ways of responding. Without attempting to deal specifically with each of these situations, here are some suggestions that I hope are closer to better than to worse.

Suggestion 1
Resolve to "be unconditionally constructive." [1]

Roger Fisher commends this resolution to secular negotiators and it's certainly fitting for Christian pastors. Being both sinful and of limited wisdom, none of us is always unconditionally constructive, but that nevertheless should be our goal. We should strive, for example, to be fair, kind, truthful, and understanding toward people we perceive as unfair, unkind, dishonest, and lacking in understanding of us. We are

to follow the Golden Rule, treating others the way we want to be treated, not the Iron Rule of treating them as they treat us. In fact, we Christians are to follow a rule even higher than the Golden Rule—we might call it the Diamond Rule—to love others as Christ loved us. There is nothing more unconditionally constructive than that!

In times of conflict we often criticize people behind their backs, but if we have complaints we should follow Matthew 18:15 and speak with them directly. This guards against the kind of destructive "triangulation" that Edwin H. Friedman repeatedly warns against in *From Generation to Generation*.[2] It also reminds us of the realism of Benjamin Franklin, who said, "Three people can keep a secret if two of them are dead!" Criticism shared in confidence has an amazing ability to reach the people we complain about. The result is often broken relationships and diminished ministry. This is true, also, of staff relationships. We should never complain to staff about other staff members. Sarcasm and put-down humor are also destructive. As Luther stated in his *Small Catechism*, the commandment forbidding false witness means that we are to speak well of our neighbors and "explain actions in the kindest way." In times of congregational conflict speech is a vital part of being unconditionally constructive.

In *Antagonists in the Church*, Kenneth Haugk writes about who are so incorrigible that it may be impossible to deal with Lloyd Rediger warns pastors to beware of "clergy-killers" in gregations.[4] There are, no doubt, those of whom we shou especially when considering an invitation to serve a congr has a history of destroying its pastors. But, from my pe greater danger is in regarding some people as "the enem Haugk and Rediger, we should also read Wayne Oates's of *Troublesome People*.[5] In the spirit of Jesus, who taug enemies, Oates reminds us that we are called to care f troublesome to us. We need to learn the art of stan and feeling the hurts that may be prompting t suffering—and yes, sinful—people need our com not just our condemnation. Even if they really ar to love them as Christ loves us.

This doesn't mean we are to treat everyon ness and phony cheerfulness. There are times human sinfulness, how can any of us do less than confess to being at least a little wrong in every conflict? On the other hand, we remember that it may be as difficult to be all wrong as it is to be all right. We don't need to blame ourselves for everything. Sensing the significance of our role, we pastors may be tempted to take too much credit for things that are good and too much blame for things that are bad.

Suppose, for example, someone becomes ill and vomits on the rug while visiting with you in your office. That would be an unpleasant experience, but I doubt that you would blame yourself and feel that you were a worthless pastor. Yet, when someone, perhaps equally sick, "vomits" on us emotionally and verbally, we may blame ourselves and feel like failures.

In most conflicts there is right and wrong on both sides, and we need to focus on solving the problem and not dwell on each other's faults. We also need to remind ourselves and the congregation that we are in difficulty together. It's not just my problem or your problem; it's our problem. During his course at Harvard on coping with conflict, Roger Fisher told students of how he sometimes has persons in conflict sit side by side. He then puts a book on the coffee table before them saying, "This book represents your problem. What can each of you do to help solve it?" When the focus is on solving the problem and not on blaming each other, the prognosis is far more hopeful.

Some pastors personalize their problems by taking credit for them. I have heard pastors say, for example, "The problems in my congregation are the result of my creative ministry. Whenever there is creative ministry, there will be problems." Then they go on to compare themselves to Jesus or some famous pastor who had conflict in the early days of what is now a booming congregation. Creative ministry often causes conflict, but all conflict is not caused by creative ministry. Some of it is caused by stubborn, self-centered pastors who fail to respect and to bond with their people.

When we feel that we are being crucified with Jesus, let's remember, as noted earlier, that there were three crosses on that hill and that our troubles may not be the result of our being so Christ-like. One bishop is reported to have replied to a pastor who told of being crucified by his congregation: "My friend, I believe the trouble with you is that you are not dead yet!" When dead to our own self-pity, self-preoccupation, and self-righteousness, we can be much more lively in life-giving, compassionate caring for our people.

Suggestion 3
Take problems seriously but don't "catastrophize" every conflict.

Benjamin Franklin suggested that before marriage we should have our eyes wide open to see what we are getting into, but after getting married we should have our eyes half shut so that we don't see things that aren't worth fussing over. In the ministry, we should look closely before accepting a new call, but once we are in it we should overlook a lot of things that aren't worth a war. It is often difficult to know when to speak and when to be silent, when to challenge and when to go along. When short on common sense but long on impulsiveness, we sometimes "catastrophize" problems that would better be treated less intensely or even with benign neglect. If this is our tendency, we wisely practice restraint and may need the guidance of a mentor or help of a therapist.

I am not suggesting that we stuff our grievances and ignore problems that are bothering us. Years ago, while taking clinical pastoral education, I visited a man in the hospital who told me he was there because he couldn't get along with his pastor. "I have tried everything," he said, "but I can't do a thing about it!" When I reported this conversation to my supervisor, he replied, "But he did do something about it! He got sick!"

Whether consciously or unconsciously, we are doing something healthy or unhealthy with the stresses of life. That parishioner got sick because he didn't deal well with his pastor. Pastors who let their parishioners "get to them" can also get sick and in some cases the experience is, no doubt, mutual. Some of us "nice guy" types who keep smiling through adversity may be making ourselves sick by failing to face and cope with the difficulties troubling us.

Suggestion 4
When needed, ask for help and be open to receive it.

When we can't figure out why someone is treating us with apparent coldness or hostility, we should be bold enough to say to that person,

"I'm feeling perplexed. Please help me to understand where you are coming from."

If that fails to resolve the conflict, compassionate counsel can help us sort things out. When troubled over a parish relationship, I sought the help of a trusted counselor. After hearing my story, one of his first comments was, "You haven't had much experience dealing with a person like this, have you?" That was certainly true, and I wasn't eager for more! His reminding me that I was dealing with a troubled person whom I didn't understand very well helped me see the situation from a new and healthier perspective.

We self-sufficient clergy, like others in the helping professions, are often reluctant to seek help and may wonder if counseling and therapy will do us any good. It was certainly good for me, and I know that it has been helpful to many. Similar helpfulness can come from participation in a small clergy support group and I also recommend that to you.

You might even risk sharing your difficulties with your bishop (or similar judicatory supervisor). That can be scary! You may fear that such disclosure will be used against you, but if your bishop has some empathy with problems of parish ministry, you will receive support and encouragement. When parish conflicts are serious, it is better for you to be the first to tell the bishop rather than waiting to be invited in after the bishop has been confronted by a delegation from your congregation complaining about you and your ministry.

Beyond receiving personal help, we are often wise to seek consultation for the congregation, and especially for lay leadership. If you don't know where to turn, your bishop or similar judicatory leader, can provide suggestions. Be hopeful but realistic in your expectations. Experienced consultants, like Speed Lees and Roy Oswald of the Alban Institute, report that many congregations receive significant help, but others continue in conflict as before and, in some cases, the consultant's opening of the wound may even make it worse. When conflicts come, I often pray Reinhold Niebuhr's "Serenity Prayer":

God, give us grace to accept with serenity the things that cannot be changed, the courage to change the things that should be changed, and the wisdom to distinguish the one from the other.[8]

Even when we can only muddle through a difficult situation, we still have the great promises that assure us that God's grace is sufficient and that "As your days are so shall your strength be" (Deuteronomy 33:25).

Suggestion 5
Focus on people's desires, not their demands. [9]

This vital principle was dinned into me during a semester in Roger Fisher's class on coping with conflict. He used many examples to illustrate the importance of focusing on people's desires rather than their demands. For example, if two people are fighting over an orange. Isn't the solution obvious? Cut it in two and give half to each. But if one wants the peeling for marmalade and the other the pulp for orange juice, that's the wrong answer! When in conflict, we wisely ask, "What do you really want?" And do not assume that wants and demands are identical.

Shortly after taking Fisher's class, I had occasion to put this principle into practice. Officers of the women's group came to the church board meeting and asked that an air conditioner be installed in the kitchen. One board member responded, "It would be dumb to have stoves heating on one side of the room while an air conditioner was working on the other," and the discussion itself got quite heated. Having learned from Dr. Fisher to focus on what people desire and not what they demand, I realized that what the women really wanted was not a machine in the window but a more comfortable kitchen. By focusing on that desire we began exploring the options (such as improved ventilation and exhaust fans over the stoves) and not just an air conditioner in the window. Following some research, a satisfactory solution was worked out to create a more comfortable kitchen.

Centering on people's wants instead of the positions they have taken is extremely helpful in solving congregational conflicts. What do those who wish to relocate to a new site and those who want to expand in the present location really want? Hopefully, most want the best facility for the best price. If they share that desire, all should be strongly encouraged to refrain from taking personal positions on the issue until essential information is gathered and every option explored. Nearly everyone might then agree that it is clearly preferable to stay or to relocate. Or they might follow the example of one of our churches and decide to become a two-point parish, operating out of both sites, or to remain in the present facility and to help start a new mission congregation in the rapidly growing area. Because we are not purely rational and decide many things on the basis of our feelings, this approach is certainly no panacea for the resolution of congregational conflict, but is often immensely helpful.

In some situations, the role of the pastor (or mediator) is similar to that of an architect working with a couple who have differences over home building plans. Each had prepared a floor plan and tried to persuade the architect of its superiority over the spouse's. It would have been foolish, said Fisher, for the architect to have supported both plans and to have encouraged each of them to keep working on their own plan. This would have locked the couple more firmly into their differing plans and might have ended their marriage as well as their dreams of a new home. Being wise, the architect asked both of them to tell him what they wanted in the new home. Then he asked the couple to give him their designs and to stop working on them until they met again. At the next meeting, he presented them with one new plan that attempted to meet both their desires. Each spouse suggested specific modifications, but by working from a single plan they were able to agree on a final design. The dream house was built and harmony was restored to the marriage. A wise pastor who keeps focused on people's desires, and not just their demands, can often facilitate similar conflict resolution in the congregation.

Suggestion 6
When agreement is impossible, work for consensus.

We often equate agreement and consensus, but they are not the same. Consensus may mean agreement but it can also mean, "I don't agree, but I will not stand in the way." We often have more consensus than agreement in our political lives, both outside and inside the church. Votes are taken, some win and some lose, but all agree to do what has been decided. There will be grumbling, but progress can be made even if some people continue *inactive* opposition.

Without consensus, progress is often difficult and sometimes impossible. A cynical parishioner once told me there are three kinds of people in every church: 1) the workers who do the work; 2) the shirkers who do little of anything, and 3) the jerkers who try to pull the rug out from under what the workers are trying to do. We wish for no "jerkers" in our congregations, but we may encounter some. And dealing with them constructively can be exceedingly difficult. Our goal in such cases should be modest. Since it is unlikely that they can be moved to support what they detest, the best we can do may be to try to keep them from standing in the way.

Although it seems contrary to common sense, Ronald Heifetz may be on to something when he suggests, "An authority should protect those whom he wants to silence." [10] I believe that this applies to pastors working with critical, nonsupportive people. By providing protection we assure them of a continued place in the community. There may even be bits of wisdom mixed in with what strikes us as mostly nonsense, and we may learn something by listening to their often aggravating questions and complaints. When we express appreciation to them for something that has been helpful, we may discover that they are not quite as cantankerous as we had believed.

Consensus is especially difficult when the majority is asked to go along with the will of the minority. Many congregational constitutions require a two-thirds vote on significant issues, such as the calling of a pastor or mortgaging property. This means that 66 percent of the congregation may want to do something, but 34 percent can stop them from doing it. When feelings are intense, there can be survival and even spiritual growth if 1) the members continue to affirm and experience unity in Christ in spite of their differences and 2) most members recognize and affirm the wisdom of requiring a two-thirds vote on significant issues.

Suggestion 7
Be willing, if necessary, to let up a little.

Imagine two people having a tug-of-war across the bow of a little boat. Each is leaning far over the side, and both are pulling on the rope with all their might. Now ask yourself, "What must they do to get back into the boat without falling into the lake?" One who pulls too hard and overpowers the other goes into the lake. If either lets go, they will both be in the water. But, if one lets up just a little, and the other wants to stay dry, a series of mutual and reciprocal "letting-up-a-little" moves will eventually result in their being back in the boat together. When involved in intense congregational tugs-of-war, we do well to remember that illustration and to pray for wisdom and courage to start the reconciliation process by being the first to "let up a little."

If everyone in a conflict stubbornly refuses to move toward reconciliation, the tragic result may be illustrated by this poetic narrative:

> There once were two cats of Kilkenny.
> Each thought there was one cat too many.
> So they fought and they fit
> And they scratched and they bit
> Til except for their nails
> And the tips of their tails
> Instead of two cats
> There weren't any.

Pastors in the midst of such congregational "cat fights" can sometimes do little more than work for a truce to keep the feuding factions from destroying each other. And, if we are leading one side of the feud, we certainly need to ask ourselves, "Is the divisive destruction of this congregation what Christ wills for my ministry?"

Suggestion 8
Renounce all forms of intimidation and manipulation.

We need to resist the temptation to use our eloquence and persuasive powers to intimidate or manipulate a congregation. During early U.S. involvement in Vietnam, President Lyndon Johnson was able to get every member of Congress and all but two in the Senate to vote in favor of the Gulf of Tonkin resolution that became the authorization for that long and tragic conflict. In retrospect, many of those who supported that resolution came to believe that they had been misled by the President. Although Johnson had a temporary victory, his joy was short-lived, and the rest is history.

Like Johnson, we may be able to get the votes. But if there has been inadequate education and discussion, the premature decision may prove to be counterproductive. Strong, visionary leadership is often exactly what is needed, but deceptive intimidation and manipulation should be beneath us as Christian pastors.

When progress is slow and frustrating, remember, "We don't make the beans grow by pulling on them," and take to heart the wisdom of the Norwegian statesman Edvard Hambro, who said that politics is not just the art of the possible but "the art of making possible tomorrow what seems impossible today." With steady nurturing and education things that can't be done today may be possible tomorrow. But if that is going to happen, our enthusiasm and zeal may need to be balanced by the equally important virtues of understanding and patience.

Suggestion 9
Affirm, and sometimes restrain, leadership of the laity.

Affirmation of leading laity is especially important in times of conflict and change. We pastors shouldn't let ourselves become the point person for every controversial proposal. Wise generals don't lead the charge over every hill. I have never heard of a coach who rushed on to the field to carry the ball on a crucial play. Wise generals and coaches operate from behind the lines and on the sidelines. They strategize and plan. They teach and inspire, and we pastors have something to learn from their example.

When a congregation has come through a time of conflict, it is sometimes necessary to restrain leaders who wish to have a great celebration of unity as soon as things have quieted down. Some are quick to say, "The conflict is over. Let's celebrate and agree never to discuss it again." Even at best, conflict resolution seldom results in perfect peace and harmony. Services of reconciliation and celebration can be helpful only when they are not premature. In addition to rejoicing, there should be acknowledgement of past and continued pain in the lives of many members. Otherwise, some will feel coerced into celebration and the superficial joy will be salt in their wounds.

Even when scars of conflict remain, it is always appropriate and helpful for congregations to reaffirm their unity in Christ and to lift up a vision of a group of people who are so centered and united in Christ that they can tolerate, and even celebrate, significant diversity.

Suggestion 10
Remember that there are places to meet again.

In the midst of intense hostility and conflict, people sometimes vow to have nothing more to do with former friends, colleagues, and fellow church members whom they now regard as their enemies. I encourage everyone to remember that whatever past difficulties have been or present feelings may be, there are still places to meet again, one of the most significant things that caring pastors can do is to help bring estranged people together for such meetings.

There is a story of a woman being interviewed by a Lutheran World Relief recruiter at the close of World War II. When asked, "How will you be able to work with people who were so recently your enemies?" she replied, "We will meet at the place of tears." There are hurting people on all sides of every conflict, and while their opinions may differ, they stand together on the common ground of pain. If they will honestly acknowledge that to one another, they can meet again "at the place of tears."

The most important place of meeting for Christians is at the foot of the cross where the ground is level and where no one has stones to throw at another. We meet there at the invitation of Jesus, and whether we like it or not and in spite of all our differences, are brothers and sisters with everyone who is there with us.

Think, for example, of the Christian resolution of the conflict between Jew and Gentile, as Paul describes it in the book of Ephesians. They had been enemies for centuries, but they became one. How did it happen? The Jews didn't give in to the Gentiles, nor did the Gentiles give in to the Jews. Each become new in Christ, and in Christ they were one. The dividing wall of hostility was broken down as Christ created "one new humanity in place of the two, thus making peace" (Ephesians 2:15). They were still Jews and Gentiles. Their individuality was not taken away. As both became part of "one new humanity," each received a new identity, and in that newness they discovered that they were brothers and sisters in one family. Or think of the metaphor of the body as Paul spells out its meaning in 1 Corinthians:

> Indeed, the body does not consist of one member but of many. If the
> foot would say, "Because I am not a hand, I do not belong to the body,"

that would not make it any less a part of the body. And if the ear should say, "Because I am not an eye, I do not belong to the body," that would not make it any less a part of the body (1 Corinthians 12:14 16).

This tells us that there is to be no self-rejection in the Christian family. No one is to say, "Because I am different, I don't belong." But that's not all. Paul goes on to say, "As it is, there are many members, yet one body. The eye cannot say to the hand, 'I have no need of you,' nor again the head to the feet, 'I have no need of you'" (1 Corinthians 12:20-21). This tells us there is to be no rejection of others in the Christian family. No one can say, "Because you are different, you don't belong." In remembrance of the fact that we "are the body of Christ and individually members of it" (1 Corinthians 12:27), we have, in spite of all our diversity, a place of meeting again.

Also, ponder again the story of the loving father, the prodigal son, and the elder brother in Jesus' parable. The two brothers were estranged from one another. Perhaps the prodigal had left home because he couldn't stand his self-righteous, domineering elder brother. Then when he came home, the elder brother went into a pout and wouldn't come to the party. The father, who had compassionately welcomed the younger son home again, now with equal compassion went out to the elder brother, inviting him in and assured him of his love and reminding him gently that the prodigal is not just "this son of yours" but is also "this brother of yours" (Luke 15:30 and 32). The story is open-ended. We don't know what happened. But we do know that in their father's compassion there is a place for them to meet again.

Stories of congregational conflict are also open-ended. When in the midst of them, we don't know how they will turn out. But we do know that in the compassion of Christ there is a place for us to meet again. Encouraging, evoking, and enabling such meetings is a vital aspect of effective, life-giving ministry.

Life-Giving Pastors
Are Prophetic
as Well as Pastoral

"Let justice roll down like waters, and righteousness like an ever-flowing stream" (Amos 5:24).

"He has told you, O mortal, what is good; and what does the Lord require of you but to do justice, and to love kindness, and to walk humbly with your God?" (Micah 6:8).

The biblical call for justice, as well as charity, relates to realities close to home and far away. Which is the more Christian response to the three following situations:

1) A community has dangerous roads and a poor traffic control system. There have been many fatal and serious accidents.

  • A concerned congregation provides an ambulance to help care for accident victims.

  • A concerned congregation commissions its church council to petition governmental authorities to provide better roads and traffic control.

2) Two thousand black residents live at the edge of a white community in South Africa. They have five water spigots, a bucket system for sewage, and shabby educational facilities.

  • A concerned congregation hires a nurse to work part-time in the black community.

• A concerned congregation stages a protest march to call attention to conditions in the black community and calls for increased taxes to provide then with an adequate water and sewage system and with education for Black children comparable to their own.

3) Congress is engaged in intense debate over the government's role in welfare and education.

• A group of church and government leaders join in calling for sharply reduced welfare and education benefits and challenging the church and voluntary organizations to provide for these needs.

• A group of church and government leaders join in calling for maintaining welfare and education funding by limiting mortgage interest tax deductions to $20,000 per year and eliminating the housing-allowance exclusion for clergy.

PASTORAL AND PROPHETIC?

These scenarios invite us to ponder the place of the prophetic as well as the pastoral in Christian ministry. Pastoral ministry expresses care and concern for the people in the parish. Prophetic ministry expresses care and concern not only for those suffering injustice and oppression in the parish but also for others in the wider community and around the world. Prophetic ministry is an extension of pastoral ministry. It widens the circle of concern to include people suffering injustice far away as well as close to home and is especially interested in the causes of their suffering.

No one, to my knowledge, has suggested that the church stop doing works of charity to help suffering people. Many people, however, have urged the church and its pastors to refrain from political involvement and public proclamation on behalf of justice.

The biblical witness presents many examples of affirmed political involvement and prophetic proclamation. Moses was not sent to provide physical assistance and words of comfort to encourage the Israelites to live with patient endurance of their oppression. He was sent to Pharaoh to deliver the people from their suffering (Exodus 3:7-10). His commitment was to justice, not just charity, and his role was prophetic and not just pastoral.

Scripture even affirms acts of civil disobedience. The King of Egypt ordered the Hebrew midwives to kill all baby boys. "But the midwives feared God; they did not do as the King of Egypt commanded them, but let the boys live" (Exodus 1:17). When called before the king, they defended their behavior with a bold-faced lie and, for all this received God's blessing: "So God dealt well with the midwives; and the people multiplied and became very strong. And because the midwives feared God, he gave them families" (Exodus 1:20-21). Would those midwives have acted differently if they had known texts like Romans 13:1-7 and 1 Peter 2:13-17, which some people believe call for total submission to governmental authority? I don't think so! They recognized that in this case, such obedience would have been sinful and idolatrous. They had not heard the witness of Peter and the apostles, but they knew in their hearts "We must obey God rather than any human authority" (Acts 5:29).

When urging Christians to refrain from challenging the authority of the state, many quote Jesus' statement, "Render to Caesar the things that are Caesar's," without also quoting, "And to God the things that are God's" (Matthew 22:21). This text compels us to ask, "What belongs to Caesar and what belongs to God?" It is sometimes difficult to know for sure, but it is certainly clear from the biblical perspective that our conscience and supreme allegiance belong to God and not to Caesar! For someone to say, "I will always obey my government no matter what I am commanded to do," is not proper patriotism, but sinful idolatry!

Colin Morris believes that to understand Jesus' answer correctly we should imagine that Jesus was present at the time of Hitler and that Jewish people asked him, "Is it right for us to pay taxes to Hitler or not?" and received this reply, "Give Hitler what Hitler's got coming, and give God what God's got coming!" From this perspective, says Morris, it is clear that Jesus' answer to the question about paying taxes to Caesar was "an emphatic No!"[1] In support of this interpretation, we note that one of the allegations brought against Jesus was, "We found this man perverting our nation, forbidding us to pay taxes to the emperor" (Luke 23:2). Did they base this accusation on their correct

understanding of Jesus' answer? I am not fully persuaded by this interpretation and believe that Christians should usually pay taxes, but it is
clear from Jesus and the prophetic witness of the Bible that there are
times when obedience to the will of God requires disobedience to
human authority.

CREATED FOR STEWARDSHIP

From the first declaration of human responsibility, "The Lord God
took the man and put him in the Garden of Eden to till it and keep it"
(Genesis 2:15), and through the rest of Scripture it is clear that we are
created to be stewards of life and of all God's gifts that enable and
fulfill life. "Think of us in this way," says the apostle Paul, "as servants
of Christ and stewards of God's mysteries. Moreover, it is required
of stewards that they be found trustworthy" (1 Corinthians 4:1-2).
The fulfillment of that stewardship certainly involves commitment to
charity—the providing of loving care to alleviate hunger, pain,
and suffering. But it also involves commitment to justice—liberation
from oppression, illness, ignorance, and all that causes human
suffering. Like Moses, we are to sometimes confront human authority
with the command of God to liberate oppressed people. As with Peter
and the apostles there may be times when we, too, must reject human
authority in order to affirm God's authority.

This is especially difficult when the majority of opinion in church
and community affirms the human authority that we believe is acting
unjustly. Our job in such situations is not just to confront the unjust
authority but to seek to transform congregational and, if possible, public opinion. Walter Brueggemann presents a concise and compelling
description of the challenge we face:

> The task of prophetic ministry is to nurture, nourish and evoke a
> consciousness and perception alternative to the consciousness and
> perception of the dominant culture around us. . . . Prophetic ministry
> consists in offering an alternative perception of reality and in letting
> people see their own history in the light of God's freedom and his
> will for justice.[2]

The task and challenge of the prophetic pastor is to offer "an alternative perception of reality" corrective of the erroneous "consciousness and perception of the dominant culture around us."

Even if we accept this challenge and agree that for Christian pastors stewardship of life and God's good gifts involves prophetic as well as pastoral ministry, the question remains, "How do we live it out?" What is the role of the pastor? Of the laity? Of the congregation? Of councils of churches? Of denominations? Commitment to justice as well as mercy does not automatically answer these questions. After decades of wrestling with these concerns, I still have no easy answers. Our response in times of crisis and controversy involves strategic and tactical considerations as well as good intentions. What is wise and right in one situation may be foolish and wrong in another.

Without offering easy prescriptions, I will share some of what I have learned through my attempt to be faithful to Christ's call to pastoral/prophetic ministry. I'll begin by telling you a little of the story that has shaped these convictions.

ANOTHER SLICE OF MY STORY

My earliest childhood memory of a pastor preaching on a social issue involved the question of whether our community should have a municipal liquor store. The preacher opposed it, as everyone apparently had expected and affirmed. Had he remained silent, some would have considered it a failure of proper ministry. I recall one man saying, "I vote dry, but I drink wet!"—and even he seemed to support the pastor's prophetic denunciation of alcohol.

When a housing development opened at the edge of the community served by my first parish, I learned of a petition to exclude black residents. About the same time, a major development opened ten miles away, and I was told that when black people approached the office a "CLOSED" sign appeared and the agent left via the back door. All the parishioners with whom I visited opposed these practices. The petition got nowhere, and black families were soon able to purchase homes in the larger development. There was no controversy in our congregation, and all that I had to do was to appreciate and affirm the leadership of our laity.

107

Then came the Vietnam War, which I opposed from the beginning. In conversations with church members I did not hide my convictions, but I did not initially preach about it. Before long, however, a time came when I was moved to say in a sermon that I did not believe that this war was the will of God and the way of Christ, and that my conscience compelled me to speak against it. I recall stating that "I hope I am wrong" and that I took no delight in the thought that the country I loved was involved in a war that I believed unwise and immoral. In that sermon, I invited members to meet with me to share their convictions and promised that I would listen respectfully.

Several days later the parish hall was filled. It was a tense and difficult meeting, not only for me but for many others, including several families of young men serving in Vietnam. But the congregation held together. No one left nor, to my knowledge, reduced their involvement or financial support.

In the summer of 1968 I joined the faculty of Luther Theological Seminary in St. Paul, and with many students and some faculty members participated in several anti-war marches and peace rallies. I also became a member of a small sharing/prayer group of seminary faculty, including an elderly professor who was a refugee from Latvia and whose family had suffered under Soviet tyranny. Our views of the Vietnam War were diametrically opposed. He saw the United States as like Christ, going to the cross to save the world from godless Communism. From my perspective, the suffering and death we were inflicting on the Vietnamese was more akin to our nailing Christ to the cross. When I shared my opinion, the elderly professor became so upset that he got up to leave the room, which prompted our unofficial leader to exclaim, "Come back and sit down!" As if struck by the voice of God, the professor returned to his place and the discussion continued. Then we all joined hands and prayed for wisdom to know God's will, and for the love to care for and respect each other in spite of our intense differences. Even after all these years that experience is still, for me, a moving example of unity in Christ in spite of significant diversity.

After five years on the seminary faculty, I was called to be senior pastor at University Lutheran Church of Hope. During my decade in that parish, I became increasingly convinced that stewardship of life required a consistent life-affirming ethic. Those convictions found expression in teaching and preaching, and in my book *Pro-Life/ Pro-Peace: Life Affirming Alternatives to Abortion, War, Mercy-Killing and the Death Penalty*, in which I took a stand against those institutions of death while at the same time granting that there are tragic exceptional circumstances when the taking of life may be justifiable.[3] Pro-choice people didn't like my pro-life stand against abortion. Pure pro-lifers, such as leaders of Lutherans for Life, rejected it because I acknowledged the possibility of justifiable abortion in the cases of rape, incest, and tragic fetal deformity. Many moderate, as well as conservative, pro-lifers didn't like my opposition to war and capital punishment, and some of my "peacenik" friends encouraged me to "have nothing to do with those pro-lifers." Nevertheless, I continued to hold these convictions.

For me as a steward of life, the escalating arms race increasingly became a matter of great concern. To possess and threaten to use nuclear, chemical, and biological weapons that could destroy civilization and possibly terminate humanity struck me as immoral idolatry. Were we really willing to save America by destroying the world? When I shared these convictions in forums and sermons interesting conversations resulted. I remember one advocate of "peace through strength" saying as he shook my hand following worship, "Well, I'm glad you got that off your chest." Another said with obvious disagreement, "I think you are sincere." But, again, I do not recall anyone leaving the congregation or reducing support.

The most intense social-issue controversies with which I have been involved concerned human sexuality. There were several out-of-the-closet gay and lesbian people at University Lutheran Church of Hope, and they seemed to be welcomed and well-received. I recall preaching a sermon series on the Ten Commandments in which I confessed to believe that our sexual orientation is discovered, not chosen, and that we should affirm human and civil rights for all people irrespective of involuntary conditions of life including sexual orientation, and that sexual morality involves the nature of our relationships, and not just kinds of sexual activity. These sermons were later developed into a book of essays called *Ten for Our Time: A New Look at the Ten Commandments*, in which I stated, as I had in one of the sermons:

Whatever our sexual orientation, we are to live responsibility and morally with the desires we have received. When we begin to understand homosexuality, we are forced to ask, "Should people of homo sexual orientation be judged by different standards than those who are heterosexual?" Sexual morality is not just a matter of actions; it is a matter of relationships, commitment, loyalty, and love. Certainly there are sinful homosexual, as well as heterosexual, relationships, attitudes, and actions. Can there also be moral sexual relationships between committed and loving persons of homosexual, as well as heterosexual, orientation? The biblical passages which clearly condemn lustful and exploitative homosexual behavior do not speak directly to this question. Some, who are deeply committed to Jesus Christ, confess to having found meaning and fulfillment in such relationships, which they believe would be impossible with persons of the opposite sex. They may be mistaken. To hear them sincerely thank God for such fulfillment may shock and disturb us, but it can also help us to be more compassionately understanding and less self-righteously judgmental.[4]

Since I did not affirm blessing of same-sex relationships or the ordination of practicing homosexuals, some may have been disappointed. Others likely felt that by even opening the door to the possibility of moral sexual relationships between committed and loving people of homosexual orientation I had gone too far, but neither the sermons nor the book evoked significant controversy.

When the first draft of the Evangelical Lutheran Church in America's statement on "The Church and Human Sexuality: A Lutheran Perspective" created headlines across the country in October 1993, intense controversy erupted. As a member of the task force that wrote it, I received several hundred telephone calls and angry letters. Some said they were leaving the ELCA, others threatened to leave or to withhold contributions. On the positive side, there were also many expressions of appreciation for a statement that, I continue to believe, is modest and moderate in its perspectives. During the following months I met with many groups, large and small, that must have included nearly 3,000 people. I came away from each of those meetings with gratitude for the way in which we were able to have respectful speaking, listening, and learning concerning the complex and controversial issues of human sexuality. I don't know what that statement may have cost the church in terms of membership and financial contributions, but I am convinced it created a great educational moment that helped reduce ignorance and increase insight among our people. I also believe that if it saved even one gay or lesbian person from despair and hopelessness that would have resulted in their giving up on the church or God or life itself, the financial cost was worth it!

Three other social issues have been part of my concern and preaching but none of them has generated much controversy: 1) our idolatrous materialistic preoccupation with money and material things, 2) our failure to care for the earth and its resources, and 3) gambling.

Like the man who voted dry but drank wet, some of our parishioners expect us to denounce materialism and affirm the care of the earth. They then go on living their materialistic and wasteful lives aware that we, who are their pastors, aren't living much differently ourselves! If our preaching and teaching on those issues has little impact, it may be because we don't practice what we preach and are more like chameleons than we are like Christ. If the love of Christ really controlled both our living and our preaching, we would be better models of financial stewardship for our people and would probably be involved in a lot of creative controversy!

Concerning gambling, I frequently quote Tolstoy's insight that gambling is immoral because the gambler's expectation of success is based upon the expectation of the misfortune of others. Gambling is inherently different from legitimate business, even risky business. Nobody has to lose for someone to make money in the stock market. A thriving company, for example, could theoretically have rising stock prices and steady dividends for a hundred years with nobody losing anything. Not so for gambling. For a few to win, many must lose! If I hope to win a million, I'm really hoping that others will have the misfortune of losing a million. Since the chances of winning the "big one" are so slim, I also believe that state lotteries are correctly described as "a tax on stupidity."

I have shared these convictions in my preaching and teaching, and in this regard, at least, practice what I preach. Some, who believe that gambling in moderation is innocent recreation, have disagreed.

But there has been no controversy, and I wonder if anyone has been persuaded to refrain from gambling.

After testifying at Minnesota House and Senate committees against expansion of gambling via video games in bars and restaurants, I received accolades of appreciation from some in the Native American community for whom that expansion would have meant increased competition with their casinos. When I explained that I was also against casino gambling, they smiled and said they knew that but were still grateful.

This experience illustrates the dilemma we often face when dealing with controversial social issues. The options are not between pure good and total evil, and the best we can do may be to encourage small steps in the right direction, or in this case, discourage small steps in the wrong direction.

LEARNINGS FOR YOUR CONSIDERATION

If what I have sketched in this personal story can be called prophetic, I believe that my ministry has been at least 90 percent pastoral and less than 10 percent prophetic. I am not bragging about that division of emphasis. In retrospect, I see my prophetic ministry as modest at best, timid at worst, and I do not present myself as a model for others to emulate.

At the same time, I am a survivor who has tried to be faithful to Christ's call to pastoral and prophetic ministry, and I believe I have learned some things worth sharing.

1.

Life-giving ministry is prophetic as well as pastoral.

Both are expressions of care for people. Note again, as emphasized earlier, the prophetic is an extension of the pastoral. Dealing with vital and often controversial issues is part of every pastor's responsibility. We are called to witness to the way of Christ, and we are not to be like weather vanes that only reflect the conditions in which we live. We are to be more like thermostats than thermometers. Pastors, as well as politicians, do well to heed the words of Edmund Burke, who said,

"Elected representatives owe their constituents not only their industry but also their judgment, and they betray rather than serve them when they sacrifice it to their opinion." Even when it is contrary to the mind of the congregation (and even of the preacher), we are called to preach the mind of Christ. Note again this challenge from Walter Brueggemann: "The task of prophetic ministry is to nurture, nourish and evoke a consciousness of perception alternative to the consciousness of perception of the dominant culture around us." [5] The biblical witness is emphatic: "Let justice roll down like waters, and righteousness like an ever-flowing stream" (Amos 5:24). To bless life-degrading evil and injustice by speech or silence is to be less than fully life-giving in our ministry.

2.

In prophetic ministry, as in dealing with conflict, it is essential that we proclaim a vision of a church so centered and united in Jesus Christ that we can stand together in whole-hearted support of the work and witness of Christ, even when differing on significant issues.

In our ministries we need to emphasize again and again that our unity is in Christ, not in the uniformity of our opinions and that, while we are many in our diversity, we are still one in Christ.

All congregations live out this vision to some extent. It is a fact of life that pro-life and pro-choice people, advocates and opponents of capital punishment, pacifists and people affirming peace through strength, smokers and anti-smokers, gamblers and non-gamblers, alcohol users and teetotalers sit side by side at worship and work together in the life of the church. If we, their pastors, have convictions on these subjects, we obviously can't agree with all of these people.

When asked his opinion on a controversial issue, one politician is supposed to have replied, "Half my friends are for it, and half my friends are against it, and I'm for my friends." That's a cute and clever answer, but it won't work very long for either politicians or pastors. When confronted with differences with our people, it is always well to remember and sometimes to say, "We're united in Christ but differ on this matter. We agree in the gospel but differ on this particular issue."

Such differences need not, and should not, keep us from working together to proclaim the gospel locally and globally.

Some sins against humanity are so abominable in their life-destructiveness that Christians have felt compelled to separate themselves from fellow believers who support them. This was true of the Confessing Church in Germany in relation to Adolf Hitler and the Holocaust. A few Lutheran congregations in South Africa were removed from fellowship with the larger church because they supported apartheid. During the height of the arms race, some Christians believed they could not be in fellowship with those who advocated the building and use of weapons that could annihilate humanity. But most issues, however strongly we may personally feel about them, do not warrant our separation from Christians whose opinions differ from our own.

3.
When dealing with controversial issues, it is essential that we stand together on common ground.

The center of that common ground is Jesus Christ. But if we are a biblical church, it also includes the Bible. If we are a confessional church, our confessions. If we are a church with traditions, our historic convictions. When dealing with controversial issues, we do not speak as politicians, but as pastors. We seek to shed the light of Scripture on the issue at hand and to share our reflections theologically and ethically, not just politically.

For me this means affirmation of Christian stewardship of life. When dealing, for example, with the issue of nuclear war I often shared Dr. Helen Caldecott's recommendation that each of us should periodically look into the starry night and ask ourselves, "Is there any other life in this vast universe?" We don't know the answer to that question, but it is possible that the thinking, loving, praying life of this planet is the only such life in all the universe. We are stewards of that life! This doesn't answer all questions concerning nuclear armaments and nuclear war but it does, I believe, help to put these issues in theological, ethical and not just political, perspective.

When dealing with controversial issues we rightly ask, "What does the Bible say?" remembering that the Bible is not a book of pat answers to every current controversy. It is not sufficient to lift up a few "proof texts." Responsible biblical interpretation always remembers that Christ, who is Lord of all, is also Lord of the Bible and requires study of text and context and of passages that speak indirectly as well as directly to the issue.

When wrestling with ethical issues, I find this statement from the apostle Paul helpful in establishing Christian common ground on which we stand together:

Owe no one anything, except to love one another; for the one who loves another has fulfilled the law. The commandments "You shall not commit adultery; you shall not murder; you shall not steal; you shall not covet;" and any other commandment are summed up in this word. "Love your neighbor as yourself." Love does no wrong to a neighbor; therefore love is the fulfilling of the law (Romans 13:8-10).

Here we see that sin is anti-love and anti life. Sin is sand in the gears of life and ultimately denies, degrades, and destroys life. Love, on the other hand, is life-affirming and life enabling. Love creates and sustains life. I have discovered that when we stand together on the common ground of this mutual understanding of sin and of love, we can have fruitful discussion of controversial issues that is otherwise often impossible.

4.

When dealing with controversial issues, we wisely heed the wisdom of James: ". . . let everyone be quick to listen, slow to speak, slow to anger" (James 1:19).

Much listening and learning should proceed our speaking on complex and controversial matters. Pastor Richard Vangerud has suggested that when denominations merge, the new church shouldn't deal with anything controversial for at least ten years. Because vital issues force themselves on us, neither denominations nor congregations nor pastors have the luxury of following Vangerud's advice, but it is still worth remembering. It is especially important that pastors new to their congregations try to postpone heavy involvement in controversial issues for at least a year. This gives time for the bonding that is so essential for effective ministry.

In both of my parish ministries I was fortunate to have had time for bonding before any red-hot issues erupted. Many are not so lucky. Parishioners may press us to affirm their convictions on a controversial issue soon after we arrive. If we agree, it may be OK to say so, but we should be aware of the fact that this information may be ammunition in a congregational civil war. However we respond when asked our view on a controversial issue, we do well to indicate that we intend to begin our ministry by focusing on Christ and the gospel and that we see ourselves as pastor to all of the parish, including those with differing opinions. Most Christians will agree that it is well for their pastors to put first things first and to care for everyone in the congregational family. Being kind and compassionate toward people who seem to affirm sins and injustices that we feel compelled to confront is not easy, but it should be a goal of our ministry.

5.
Remember that taking controversial stands changes how people think of us as well as of the issues.

For example, I am opposed to capital punishment. I don't think that we show that it is wrong to kill people by killing people. If we oppose killing by killing, should we also oppose torture by torturing and rape by raping? I believe that when Jesus stopped an execution and said, "Let anyone among you who is without sin be the first to throw a stone at her" (John 8:7), he abolished capital punishment. What is your reaction to my sharing these convictions? Perhaps it shifted your opinion concerning the death penalty, or it may have changed your opinion of me. If you are a strongly committed supporter of capital punishment, you now think less of me and question my ability to make good judgments. If you are a crusader against the death penalty, you may now think more highly of me and have an enhanced opinion of my wisdom.

Awareness of the way in which our stands on controversial issues affect how people regard us as persons and pastors should not panic us into silence, but it can help us be more understanding of other people and more sensitive to their needs. It is also another reminder of the importance of having sufficient "credit" in our "bonding bank" so that we don't go broke when we take stands on controversial issues.

6.
When dealing with controversial subjects, it is essential that we thoroughly understand the issues and the perspectives of our people.

Understanding requires learning, and learning requires serious study, reflection, and much listening. None of us should pontificate about things we don't understand, and we should not presume to understand things we have not carefully studied. It is especially important that we do not intentionally, or because of misunderstanding, misrepresent the positions of those with whom we disagree. Here again, we practice the Golden Rule: because we dislike being misrepresented, we will not misrepresent others. In debate on controversial issues, we should seek to state our opponents' positions fairly so they will be able to say, "Yes, that's what I believe."

We should also acknowledge the best, and not just attack the worst, arguments in favor of our opponent's perspective. Demolishing ten dumb reasons for doing something proves nothing if there is still one excellent reason to do it. There are even times when it's helpful to bring up evidence and arguments in support of the opposition's case that their presenters fail to mention. This demonstrates our fairness and gives us further opportunity to explain why, in spite of everything that can be said on behalf of another perspective, ours is the wiser course.

7.
It is often wise to follow a deliberate process of prophetic ministry in the parish.

Begin with conversation with individuals you respect. Confess that you have struggled with the issue and that these are your developing convictions. Ask them to share their reactions and sincerely seek to learn from one another. Then raise the issue in adult forums and Bible class discussions. In these conversations, always share your convictions as a confession, not an attack. Saying, "You are wrong," and saying, "I see that differently," convey the same message but a different attitude

117

and impression. The first prompts an angry, defensive response; the second encourages the person to say, "Tell me how you see it." The first creates conflict; the second invites listening and learning.

Preaching on controversial issues should generally follow much personal conversation and small-group discussion. This demonstrates that our preached convictions arise from serious study, reflection, and deliberation. It's not much fun to deal with surprised church members who are shocked by preached opinions contrary to their own. Even when something happens that is of such significance that it demands immediate comment in a sermon, it is often well to share what you intend to say with a few trusted individuals or a small group of your leaders to learn from their reactions. Usually we will be affirmed by their encouragement, but even if not, we will be wiser and more firmly bonded with these people than we would have been if we had not met together.

In denominations like mine, where most of the preaching is based on the lectionary of Bible texts, I believe it is generally wise to deal with controversial issues when the light of those texts falls upon them rather than to select that subject as the sermon topic. However, there are times when topical sermons and even a whole series of sermons can seek to shed the light of Christ and the Bible on specific social and political concerns.

8.

When dealing with controversial issues, it is important to acknowledge that "I could be wrong" and in some instances to say, "I hope I am wrong."

Paul Scherer warned us against being "the kind of preachers who stand in the pulpit four feet above contradiction and look down on their people." We are seldom as tempted toward self-righteousness as when we are absolutely convinced of the correctness of our convictions and of the stupidity and sinfulness of those with whom we disagree. At such times it is easy for us to be wrong in our attitudes, even while right in our opinions.

I recall counseling with a man years ago to whom I finally said, "I think you are going to have to choose between being right and being married." He told me later that "I know that if I'd been less arrogant and domineering, we'd still be married, but I just couldn't do it!" Similarly, those of us with strong and clear convictions may sometimes have to choose between being right about everything and being pastors of the congregation we are called to serve. This doesn't mean that we have to compromise our convictions, but it may mean that we need to be humble enough to acknowledge that we could be wrong and that we still have something to learn.

Some wonder why anyone would ever say, "I hope I am wrong," especially when preaching and teaching. But, don't we often hope we are wrong? If I have symptoms that convince me that I have cancer, I hope I'm wrong. Similarly, if I believe that millions of abortions involving the slaughter of the innocent are a holocaust comparable to the Nazi slaughter of the Jews, or that the execution of a criminal is legalized murder, or that a particular war is contrary to the will of God and the way of Christ, I can still hope that I am wrong. Because these things are happening, it would, needless to say, be a great relief to learn that I was mistaken and that these activities were blessed by God. Confessing that "I may be wrong" or that "I hope I am wrong" is not the same as saying, "I think I am wrong." But such acknowledgements help save us from self-righteousness and invite further discussion and deepened bonding with our people.

9.
**After having taken a stand on a controversial issue,
it is essential to invite response and reaction from our people.**

If there are feedback cards in the pews, they will provide a means of immediate response. If a small group is meeting regularly with the pastor for discussion of preaching, we will have the opportunity for extended conversation. Beyond that it is often wise to invite both those who agree and disagree to meet at a specific time and place for further discussion. In every possible way we should seek to provide security, protection, and honest affirmation for those whose opinions differ from our own so they will not feel isolated and rejected.

It may even be wise to invite someone to give a "temple talk" presentation or even to preach the sermon on another Sunday, expressing views contrary to our own. This can, of course, be dangerous. That person may be more eloquent and persuasive than we are. Or, on the other hand, if 99 percent of our people share our conviction, we may be severely criticized for inviting such an heretical, immoral person to address the congregation. In such cases, it is probably better to invite the person to share those contrary convictions at a forum or class rather than during worship. We can defend our action by telling our critics that we all need to know what others are thinking.

Unless they have been driven away, there are persons of homosexual orientation in most of our congregations. I encourage all parishes to invite gay and lesbian Christians to share their testimonies during adult forums and classes. Since gay and lesbian people, like all the rest of us, do not always agree, it may be well to have representatives of more than one group make presentations. Because this has become such a vital and volatile issue in many of our parishes, I believe that the least we can do is listen respectfully to the witnesses of brothers and sisters in Christ who have discovered themselves to be homosexual.

10.
In summary, I again emphasize the importance of reminding ourselves as well as the congregation that our unity is in Christ and not in the uniformity of our opinions.

Even after careful and respectful study, discussion, and preaching concerning a particular issue, intense differences of opinion will likely remain. But we can learn to live with our differences without beating either the subject or one another to death. When done well, discussion, teaching, and preaching will generally create sufficient consensus to enable continued worship, work, and witness together. Then the congregation learns in its own experience that it is possible to be so centered and united in Jesus Christ that people can live and serve together in spite of their differences. From my perspective, that is an immensely significant achievement. This sometimes seems beyond the capacities of pastor and people, but it is never beyond the possibilities of the grace of God. Effective, life-giving ministry can and does happen when Christ-centered clergy are both compassionately pastoral, and wisely as well as courageously prophetic.

Life-Giving Pastors
Respect Boundaries

"For everything there is a season, and a time for every matter under heaven. . . . a time to embrace, and a time to refrain from embracing" (Ecclesiastes 3:1,5).

"Shun immorality. . . . Do you not know that your body is a temple of the Holy Spirit within you, which you have from God? You are not your own; you were bought with a price. So glorify God in your body" (1 Corinthians 6:18-19 RSV).

When someone first told me of a pastor who had committed a "boundary violation," I wondered if he had driven his car into his neighbor's yard. That was about twelve years ago, and I am sorry to have to report that since then I've learned a lot about "boundary violations" and have discovered they are usually a lot more destructive than car tracks in someone's newly planted sod.

People, as well as real estate, have boundaries. There are private areas of sexual, psychological, spiritual, and social space that are not to be invaded without welcome by anyone. And even when invited, sexual boundaries are never to be transgressed by those persons in positions of power such as medical doctors, counselors, and clergy.

If I had written about the habits of life-giving pastors a dozen years ago, there probably would have been a brief reference to the importance of avoiding "conduct unbecoming to the pastoral office," as we then called it, but there would have been no chapter on boundary violations. In those days, bishops or other supervisors tried to deal pastorally with clergy guilty of "conduct unbecoming," which often meant resignation from the parish, followed by several months of intensive therapy and counseling. If the psychotherapist indicated that future transgression was unlikely, the pastor would usually be reaffirmed for call and in a few months be serving another parish. If the offense were serious, the congregation would have been told of its general nature and assured they need not fear it would happen again.

TIMES HAVE CHANGED

Those days seem to describe a world of long ago and far away. By being confronted with the tragic consequences of sexual boundary violations for both the victim and the perpetrator, we have lost both our innocence and our naïveté. We have also learned that many boundary violators are repeat offenders and that moral exhortation and competent counseling cannot guarantee that it won't happen again.

Ironically, but perhaps understandably, most of those with whom I have dealt concerning boundary violations have been among our most promising and highly esteemed pastors. They have bonded quickly with their people and have had the capacity of evoking great trust and confidence from their parishioners. This helped make their ministries effective but also increased their seductive capacity. Needless to say, it did not make their violations excusable.

One of the most significant insights now governing the church's response to clergy sexual misconduct is awareness of the role of power in pastor-parishioner relationships. I must confess that, during my years of parish ministry, I was never aware of having such seductive power and was, perhaps, blessed by my ignorance. I assumed that if I were to step across the line, sexually speaking, someone would (literally or figuratively) whack me across the head and that would be the end of it, and perhaps also of my ministry. Now I've learned that we pastors, like others in the helping professions, have more power than we realize. We may, in the eyes of some susceptible people, exude professional competence, caring, and compassion. When basking in such trusting adulation, some pastors seduce both themselves and their parishioners into sinful sexual activity.

The boundaries violated are both their own and their parishioners. Sexual misconduct involves a double transgression. It goes beyond the limits that are proper for a clergy person as a Christian and as a pastor. It also transgresses into the sacred, private space of a parishioner.

In addition, sexual misconduct undermines gospel ministry and is often devastating to the life of the congregation.

Victims of such misconduct may at first be unaware of being victimized. When looking back upon such a relationship, one pastor told me that he knew there were victims—his wife, children, and congregation were clearly victims—but he certainly did not think of the woman with whom he had been involved as a victim. She was, in his opinion, a willing and joyful participant in their sexual adventure, and at least as responsible for it as he was. When she brought legal action against him, he was finally confronted with the hurtful effects of his behavior and forced to face the fact that legally, if not morally, he was 100 percent responsible.

The destructiveness of sexual misconduct again underscores the fact that sin is anti-life. However glamorous and exhilarating it may seem at the time, sexual misconduct is ultimately life-denying and life-degrading for both pastor and parishioner, and it is utterly incompatible with life-giving ministry. In addition to the testimony of angry victims and sorrowful clergy, we can thank the legal profession for waking us up to the hurtfulness of sexual misconduct. This awakening has been shocking, painful, and costly. Even when acknowledging excessive litigation, we need to admit that it has taught us lessons we should have learned long ago without the benefit of legal instruction.

My commentary on the legal dimensions of sexual misconduct reflects my recent experience as a bishop. This emphasis, however, does not mean that the legal realities are my primary concern. My chief concerns are for the victims, for the prevention of further victimization, for pastors who have violated sacred boundaries, for the continued effectiveness of life-giving ministry, and for the well being of the congregation and wider church.

THE LEGAL REALITIES

For better or worse, and I think it is sometimes both, the legal realities are here to stay. In Minnesota, for example, we have a law that prompts most congregations to conduct background checks on every pastor who is called to serve. In our denomination, congregational presidents and pastoral colleagues are specifically asked to report evidence, and even suspicions, of sexual misconduct as specified in the law. Other states are following Minnesota's example in enacting such legislation.

Because of the imbalance of power between pastor and parishioner, the letter of the law specifies that the voluntary, willing, and even joyful participation of a parishioner in such misconduct is irrelevant and no basis for defense. As we now understand it, sexual misconduct is not only a sin; it is also a crime.

If wisdom involves consideration of consequences, it is also obvious that sexual misconduct is exceedingly unwise. It is, in fact, so foolish that Patrick Shiltz, whose entire legal practice involved defending churches against litigation, regards it as evidence that a pastor must have some very serious moral and psychological problems to take such risks. To illustrate his point, I recall that one of my seminary professors pointed out that we pastors are strongly supported in our commitment to sexual faithfulness. "Just think," he said, "of all we would lose if we were caught in sexual infidelity. We'd not only risk loss of marriage and family, but also reputation and vocation." He then suggested that we should, without condoning, be compassionate toward those who lacked such constraints and not be self-righteously judgmental.

But then what about pastors who, in spite of the immense risk of tragic consequences still become involved in sexual boundary violations? Is Shiltz correct that there must be some kind of serious underlying problem that enables a pastor to embark on such folly? I think so, and I have come to believe that sexual misconduct, even if it involves only a single incident, is a symptom of a serious malady that cannot be excused or rationalized as a relatively innocent, temporary lapse of good judgment. There are significant differences between sexual predators who have repeated involvements with many victims and the pastor who immediately recognizes a boundary violation and seeks help to prevent it from ever occurring again. But such pastoral conduct is still sufficiently serious to warrant resignation from the parish and possible withdrawal of affirmation for future pastoral ministry.

AN AGONIZING DILEMMA

It has been agonizing for me as bishop to be a proclaimer of the gospel of forgiveness and restoration while, on the other hand, having to affirm other realities that precluded continued public ministry. In this struggle I have learned that forgiveness of sins does not always mean restoration to professional responsibility. Forgiveness means that God still loves us, and it is certainly clear from the witness of Jesus that God loves sexual sinners and that they may be less reprehensible in the sight of God than self-righteous pharisees and bishops. But the fact of God's loving forgiveness does not mean that a pastor with a history of sexual abuse of children should be called to be minister of education and youth in a congregation! Forgiveness is one thing—an exceedingly important thing—but it does not automatically provide the responsible self-control that is necessary for life-giving ministry. As bishops and leaders of congregations we are to do our best to assure that sexual misconduct does not occur in our churches.

Although it seems harsh to deny renewed opportunity for ministry to one who has had a boundary violation and has received extensive therapy, such treatment cannot guarantee that there will be no further offense. In fact, the therapists and counselors with whom I have dealt seem increasingly reluctant to give assurances that such misconduct will not reoccur. This may reflect their fear of litigation, but it may also be an honest acknowledgement that present therapies cannot guarantee that a pastor has been "cured" and will not "act out" again.

Beyond concern to prevent future victimization, no denomination, bishop, or congregation can ignore the present legal realities. Some people have asked, "Why do we make such a big deal of our pastor's sexual sins? Pastors are human, too! Aren't other pastoral sins equally serious?" All of that is true, but it ignores the fact that some sins are more hurtful than others.

During a time of emotional stress, a pastor walked out of a store with a TV without paying for it. He was caught, resigned from his congregation, went through therapy, was restored to ministry, and is serving well in another parish. Hearing of this, some say, "Isn't stealing as serious as sexual sin? Why should he be restored to the ministry when a pastor guilty of sexual misconduct is denied that opportunity?" To this I reply, "Of course, stealing a TV set is sinful. But such property violations are minimal in their hurtfulness compared to the sexual violation of persons. Furthermore the legal consequences of taking a TV set are nearly nonexistent while the compensatory and punitive damages for sexual misconduct can total in the millions."

Those damages are especially severe when they involve the repeated offense of a person already known to have had a boundary violation. David Hardy, attorney for the Evangelical Lutheran Church in America, uses the illustration of a family that owns a friendly and playful dog. One day the neighbor's child steps on the dog's tail and is bitten. Since the dog was known to be safe and had never bitten anyone, there would be little legal liability for that first bite. But if the owner keeps the dog and another child is bitten, there would be great legal liability. Please don't press this analogy. Human beings are not dogs. Pastors do not get one free bite! But the main point is clear: compensatory awards, and especially punitive awards for sexual misconduct, are often far greater for subsequent offenses than for first offenses. When we consider reinstatement of a pastor following a boundary violation, our legal counsel always asks, "Are you so short of pastors that you are willing to risk the entire financial resources of this parish and of your synod to provide a call for this person?"

I believe there may be times when, in affirmation of Christ and the power of the Holy Spirit to heal and restore broken lives, we should take that risk. Unless we are willing to establish a legalistic rule that states, "Anyone who has ever been involved in any kind of sexual boundary violation will never again be considered for parish ministry in this church," we must evaluate every situation on a case-by-case basis. A legalistic rule would certainly be easier to administer, but would it reflect a gospel that not only promises forgiveness but offers hope of healing and restoration? What would you do if you were the bishop or the chair of a congregational call committee when confronted with that attorney's question and the other questions raised here?

On several occasions, I and a pastor who has transgressed sexual boundaries have met with legal counsel to discuss the implications of reinstatement to parish ministry. The attorney always points out that reinstatement sometimes precipitates a lawsuit. A victim of misconduct may be satisfied that a pastor who has been removed from the parish has been properly disciplined. But when the victim learns that the pastor is back in parish ministry, anger may be rekindled that says in effect, "Since the church has failed to adequately discipline this pastor and now risks the creation of more victims, I will personally act to stop him from serving as a pastor." The means chosen to create that result may be a lawsuit filed against the pastor, the congregation, the synod or similar jurisdiction, and the entire denomination. The damages sought, and sometimes granted, are often in the hundreds of thousands (and sometimes millions) of dollars. In such cases, it is certainly counter to the pastor's own self-interest to be restored to parish ministry.

IS IT FAIR TO BLAME ONLY THE PASTOR?

All pastors should respect sexual boundaries. Those who fail to do so are personally responsible and should accept the consequences. We are free to choose, but we are not free to choose the consequences that come from our choices. Sexual misconduct is especially reprehensible and hurtful when the victim is a vulnerable adult, youth, or child incapable of resisting pastoral power. Even if there is a measure of mutuality, there is seldom, if ever, full equality between a doctor and a patient, a counselor or a counselee, or a pastor and parishioner. The person in the position of power is 100 percent responsible to maintain professional boundaries.

This does not mean that all victims are 100 percent helpless and irresponsible. Some adults, many youth, and most children are so vulnerable that they have little, if any, responsibility for the misconduct. Others have had the strength to rebuff the first hint of boundary intrusion and have stopped it cold so that no misconduct occurred. Still others have permitted, or even invited, sexual involvement that would not have occurred if they had exercised the power they possessed to resist it. The honest acknowledgment of such moral failure does not, however, diminish by even 1 percent the fact that the pastor is still 100 percent responsible. Nothing that is said or done justifies a doctor's sexual involvement with a patient. Nothing that is said or done justifies a pastor's sexual involvement with a parishioner. The sinfulness of patients and parishioners does not excuse the sins of doctors and pastors. They must deal with their sins and we with ours.

Instead of taking advantage of vulnerable people or blaming our misconduct on the failure of others, those of us in positions of power should do all that we can to strengthen their ability to resist and prevent boundary violations. Jan Erickson-Pearson's *Safe Connections: What Parishioners Can Do to Understand and Prevent Clergy Abuse* is an excellent resource in this regard and a specific recommendation regarding its use is included later in this chapter. [1]

In retrospect, it is obvious that years ago churches should have done what they are trying to do now to alert pastors and parishioners to the tragic consequences of sexual misconduct and to provide resources for its prevention. At the same time, it strikes me as unfair that churches, which acted in accord with the best understanding available at the time, be judged by today's standards concerning violations that occurred decades ago. A lawsuit filed against one of our congregations alleged sexual misconduct in 1955! If guilty, a pastor should be disciplined by the church, but I believe it unfair to require the congregation and denomination to pay thousands of dollars of punitive damages because they did not then deal with the situation as we would today.

By way of illustration, I had polio when two years old and orthopedic surgery on my foot at ages five and seven. Following the first surgery I was hospitalized for 90 days and after the second for 109 days, all of which was very traumatic for me. No doctor today would keep a child in the hospital for more than a few days following such surgery, and I now consider those prolonged hospitalizations to have been a form of child abuse. But it was standard procedure at that time. Should I now claim to have recently realized that many of my past and present problems resulted from that abuse and then file a multi-million dollar lawsuit against the hospital? Such a lawsuit would be absurd and unfair. They did what they believed to be best according to the understanding and standards of that time.

Similarly, I believe the churches have tried to do their best to prevent further abuse and to rehabilitate clergy. Nevertheless, hundreds of thousands of dollars in punitive damages has been assessed against churches for having failed, years ago, to act by today's standards. This is especially troubling not only because there is no insurance for punitive damages but also because the punishment assumes that congregations and church leaders acted with malicious intent, which I believe to be false.

These are complex and difficult issues. Both the churches and the legal profession are struggling toward better ways of responding to sexual misconduct. This is a painful road to travel, and I hope that better ways will be found to affirm justice and fairness for all. In the meantime, these are the realities of the pastor's world and it is perilous for us to ignore or deny them.

NON-SEXUAL BOUNDARY VIOLATIONS

Before sharing some suggestions concerning how to make the best of this difficult world, I must emphasize that boundary violations do not always involve sexual misconduct. We and our parishioners are surrounded by sacred psychological, emotional, social, and spiritual space that should not be violated by pastors or anyone else. Church history tells of powerful clergy who have manipulated and abused their parishioners. The stories of Jim Jones, David Koresh, and the fictional Elmer Gantry are flagrant examples of the hurtfulness in some of our churches. Pastoral power can be used to create cultish adulation in vulnerable parishioners who become excessively dependent upon, and sometimes slavishly obedient to, the pastor. Although congregational fellowship can certainly enrich our lives, we should beware of using our parishioners to fulfill either our sexual or non-sexual needs. As followers of Jesus our primary calling is "Not to be served, but to serve," not to take but "to give" (Mark 10:45).

Congregational management by fear, intimidation, manipulation, and other forms of psychic and emotional coercion can involve boundary violations that are as serious as those that are sexual. The psychic and spiritual seduction and rape of parishioners by exploitive clergy is a reality that needs to be investigated, exposed, stopped and prevented with the same vigor with which sexual abuse and misconduct is being addressed. If that is to happen, victims must be as bold in coming forward with their reports of such abuse as have those who have been the victims of sexual misconduct and we who are in positions of leadership must be as receptive to their stories and as responsible in our response.

The most comprehensive discussion of this wide-spread and serious problem of which I am aware, is in the book *The Subtle Power of Spiritual Abuse: Recognizing and Escaping Spiritual Manipulation and False Spiritual Authority Within the Church,* by David Johnson and Jeff VanVorderen.³ A ten-tape video (or audio) series by the authors entitled "Breaking the Silence of Spiritual Abuse" is available from Damascus Inc.³ Among many examples, they tell of a pastor who abused a clinically depressed person by telling her that her depression was the result of her "rebellion against God" and who then attempted to cure her with "a 'prescription' of praise Scriptures to memorize and repeat over and over." They go on to state that:

> Spiritual abuse can occur when a leader uses his or her *spiritual position* to control or dominate another person. It often involves overriding of feelings and opinions of another, without regard to what will result in the other person's state of living, emotions or spiritual well-being. In this application, power is used to bolster the position of needs of the leader, over and above one who comes to them in need.⁴

Johnson and Van Vonderen are specifically critical of instances when shame was used in an attempt to get someone to support a belief or to fend off legitimate questions. They give a warning to each of us by saying:

> When your words and actions tear down another, or attack or weaken a person's standing as a Christian—to gratify you, your position or your beliefs while at the same time weakening or harming another—that is spiritual abuse.⁵

Another form of boundary violation involves pastors inappropriate involvement in parishes they have previously served. For pastors to continue to be members of the congregation they served is not always a problem. My predecessor and his family were members of my second parish, and I know of a large congregation where almost all the previous pastors, together with about twenty-five other clergy, are members and there have been no difficulties of which I am aware. Nevertheless, my experience as a bishop has taught that it is usually best for everyone involved, including the previous pastor, that ties be clearly cut and membership established elsewhere.

If the previous pastor continues to reside in the community, he or she should be emphatic in indicating support for the new pastor by refusing to do any pastoral acts in the parish except at the specific invitation of the present pastor. Nor should the departing pastor respond to invitations to do pastoral acts by saying, "I'll be glad to if the present pastor invites me." Such comments are really cheap shots that unfairly put the present pastor on the spot. What is she or he then to say? It is far better for the previous pastor when invited to perform a wedding, for example, to encourage the couple to contact the present pastor and, if desired, to welcome an invitation to attend as a guest. The parish is now the new pastor's territory and, except for special occasions and invitations initiated by the present pastor, previous pastors are generally wise to move out and stay out!

On the other hand, new pastors need not be excessively defensive of their "territory." If a former pastor continues to maintain a few friendships with members of your parish, it is usually best to accept it graciously. You may someday discover that you are doing the same thing—perhaps even with the same people!

SOME STRONG RECOMMENDATIONS

In earlier chapters I have shared suggestions and learnings for your consideration. In this chapter I will be more directive and make some strong recommendations. I present them emphatically because I believe that we ignore them at our peril and at the peril of our people and our parishes.

Suggestion 1

Face the fact that boundary violations, sexual and otherwise, are sinful, wrong, unprofessional, and destructive of life-giving ministry.

Suggestion 2

Take the lead in teaching the members of your congregation, young and old alike, to respect the boundaries of others and to resist transgression of their boundaries. Tell them, "If I or anyone on our staff, or any lay volunteer, ever says or does anything that you find inappropriate or invasive, tell us to stop it, and insist that we do so." There is a model for such emphatic candor in the New Testament: "Even if we or an angel from heaven proclaim to you a gospel contrary to what we proclaim to you, let that one be accursed!" (Galatians 1:9). Paul told the Galatians to reject a false gospel, even if he preached it himself! So also, we should tell our people to reject sinful misconduct, even if it comes from us or from someone who looks like "an angel from heaven."

In addition to sharing such a statement in every possible way with everyone in your congregational family, including children and youth, encourage your people to read and discuss *Safe Connections: What Parishioners Can Do to Understand and Prevent Clergy Sexual Abuse*, by Jan Erickson-Pearson. Use some of your pastoral power to make it required reading for all staff and lay volunteers and encourage its use as a resource for meetings of your church women's group, men's group, and youth group. Ask your church school teachers to instruct their students to respect boundaries, and to resist, and to report attempts to invade their boundaries. Remember that in the case of boundary violations, an ounce of prevention is worth far more than a pound of cure. (Perhaps it's closer to a ton?)

Suggestion 3

Accept the fact that the willingness, or even seductive advances, of a parishioner do not excuse sexual misconduct. We are 100 percent responsible for our actions and for setting our own boundaries!

Suggestion 4

Make an absolute commitment to refrain from testing, let alone transgressing, any sexual, psychological, emotional, or spiritual boundary. Resolve in every situation to act with the kind of love that "does no wrong to a neighbor" (Romans 13:10).

Suggestion 5

Be alert to warning signs that may indicate that you are vulnerable to temptations to violate boundaries. These include, suffering from fatigue and burnout, feeling sorry for ourselves, feeling unappreciated, harboring resentments toward our family or congregation, having marital problems, working long hours in order to stay away from home, feeling depression, anxiety, and apathy, having a compulsive need to exercise authority to make the congregation successful, failing to take a weekly day off or use vacation time, using the church to satisfy a majority of personal and social needs.

Specific indications that we may be on a slippery slope, sliding toward sexual misconduct include, having strong sexual attraction and frequent erotic fantasies and daydreams concerning a parishioner, frequently telephoning and visiting with a parishioner for personal enjoyment, creating work-related excuses to spend time alone together, coming to regard a parishioner as a very special friend, excessive personal sharing of problems and feelings, telling of our special fondness for someone, giving and receiving personal gifts, hugging and holding for personal enjoyment, sharing secrets with each other, wishing that our spouse were more like this special person, thinking and telling that such a wonderful relationship is a special gift from God, subtle (or not so subtle) sexual conversation and behavior.

Suggestion 6

If such signs persist, it is essential that we have a mentor, counselor, or therapist with whom to share our feelings and concerns. If we are, for example, caught up in a fantasy concerning a parishioner, or a parishioner expresses romantic interest in us, we should seek the help of a competent outsider as quickly as possible. Martin Luther said, "We can't keep the birds from flying over our heads, but we can stop them from making nests in our hair." When the fantasies are getting frequent and the birds are looking for a place to nest, we need help and should not delay in getting it. If tempted to risk our vocation, reputation, and family for a romantic escapade, we have deep problems and should not kid ourselves into thinking that we can handle it alone. Realize that you are already in the frying pan and take action that keeps you from falling into the fire!

Suggestion 7

Be exceedingly reserved with regard to all physical touching and hugging. I cannot recommend that we never touch or hug anyone. There is

"A time to embrace, and a time to refrain from embracing" (Ecclesiastes 3:5). Imagine, for example, being in a hospital waiting room with a family whose son is in surgery after a tragic car accident. After several hours the doctor reports, "I'm sorry, we were unable to save your son." Should the only physical touching be handshakes with the family? Such reserve would be callous rejection at a time when hugging and holding would be clearly appropriate. This is, however, an extreme situation, and it is best that our hugging and holding be exceptional and occasional and not frequent and casual.

I don't recall having refused to hug anyone, but I am now more reserved about initiating hugs than I used to be. I also recommend opening the office door at the close of a counseling session and stepping out into the hallway so that any hugging that occurs will be in public and not in private space. We need to be alert to our motives for such physical contact. Hugs that comfort a grieving person are one thing. Hugging and holding parishioners for self-gratification is something else and is, from my perspective, already over the edge of sexual misconduct. We are wise to stop before it goes further.

Suggestion 8

Beware of prolonged counseling in private, especially when alone at the church or in a person's home. Having done a lot of private office counseling and home visitation during my twenty years in the parish without any boundary violation problems, I continue to affirm private pastoral counseling behind a closed door and visitation of parishioners in their homes. But because I have been out of the parish for a dozen years, this perspective may be out of date. To me, the essential boundary setting is done in the pastor's head and heart, and if that is clear and firm, we need not act as if someone is out to seduce us or as if we are living on the edge of loss of self-control. But we do need to beware and be exceedingly discreet. It is essential that we refrain from counseling and visitation that it is done primarily for our self gratification and not to benefit of the parishioner. If there is any doubt in this regard, we should probably not do it.

I recently visited a new church that had a window of clear glass at the side of each pastor's door so that anyone walking by could look inside. I was told that this had been done to protect the pastors. Perhaps this reflects what the pastoral world has come to, but I don't want people looking through a window into my office. I also fear that it would prompt parishioners to stay away or to suggest that we meet somewhere else that might be a far worse setting! We certainly need to stay clear of any situation or circumstance that tempts ourselves or a parishioner toward misconduct, but we need not be so preoccupied with precautions that we, in effect, hang a sign on our office door that says, "Beware, I can't be trusted!" It is tragically true that there are some pastors for whom such a sign is appropriate, but I continue to believe that the overwhelming majority clearly recognize and responsibly respect boundaries.

Suggestion 9

During pastoral counseling, beware of probing for details to satisfy your prurient interest and of excessive personal sharing, especially of a sexual nature. Deciding what to ask and what to share is often difficult. In marriage counseling I was sometimes too reserved in my questioning and failed to learn, until far later than I should have known, of sexual problems that were troubling the marriage. There were probably other occasions when I asked for more than I needed to know.

As indicated earlier, I believe there are times when it is appropriate for a pastor to share experiences similar to those of a counselee. If told, for example, of the miseries of a long childhood hospitalization, I believe it would be helpful for me to tell a little of my story. But, if a woman told of feeling lonely and rejected by her husband, it would be utterly inappropriate for a pastor to confess to similar feelings toward a spouse. The key to what we ask and what we share is whether or not it is for the benefit of the parishioner. We should never use our counselees to satisfy our own needs. That should never be the motive for continuing a counseling relationship. If we need therapy or love or friendship, we should seek it elsewhere than from a counselee!

Suggestion 10

When sexually attracted to a parishioner or counselee, we should never confess that fact to the person to whom we are attracted. The only exception to this rule might be if both pastor and parishioner are single and they wish to start a dating relationship. In that case, the counseling should be referred to someone else, and it might even be best that the parishioner join another congregation.

In light of all the happy marriages that had their romantic beginnings in the attraction of single pastors and parishioners, this recommendation may seem excessive, but we need to beware of the dangers involved. For instance, according to Patrick Shiltz, the following scenario is possible under Minnesota law: A pastor and parishioner, both single, fall in love during a counseling relationship. They begin dating and six months later they are married. Problems develop in the marriage and after a year she files for divorce. Then, even though that had no sexual relations prior to marriage, she sues the pastor for having seduced her into marriage through the manipulative use of power during the counselor-counselee relationship. Far out? To be sure! But possible! Therefore, beware!

Suggestion 11

When a parishioner confesses sexual attraction or romantic feelings toward the pastor, we should respond by clearly affirming responsible boundaries. This will require candid conversation that continues to affirm our care for the person but at the same time rejects any possibility of sexual involvement. It may be best to acknowledge that sometimes such feelings develop in counseling and that it is safe to talk about them because you adhere to a sacred rule and never have sexual involvement with counselees. If personal attraction continues to be a theme in the counseling, and especially if you begin to have reciprocal feelings yourself, it is essential that the counseling relationship be terminated with referral to another counselor.

When a counselee develops sexual feelings toward you, don't tell your spouse. To do so is a violation of pastoral confidence and a serious breach of professional ethics. Such information is none of your spouse's business! But if you are having trouble dealing with it, you should share it with a mentor or counselor, but without identifying the person being counseled. While not a breach of confidence, since you would be telling about yourself and not of what had been confided by a parishioner, informing your spouse of your attraction toward a parishioner also strikes me as unnecessary and unwise. Although we all yearn for marriages in which we can share everything in open and honest intimacy, there are some things better not shared. What would be the purpose of such sharing? It would be true, but would it be kind? It would be honest, but would it be helpful? If we need a therapist or a counselor, it should be someone other than our spouse. The role of husband or wife is sufficiently challenging without adding the role of counselor and therapist.

"But," you may wondering, "what if my spouse asks me? Am I to lie?" If that happens, I believe you should honestly acknowledge that you find that person, along with many others, to be attractive and that you enjoy their company but that there has not been and never will be any inappropriate behavior between you. If there is no question about the latter, there should be no problem in being honest about the former!

Suggestion 12

If some form of sexual misconduct is part of your personal history and it has never become known, be absolutely certain you have dealt with it, both confessionally and therapeutically. If there is the slightest chance that you might act out again, get the help you need and, if necessary, remove yourself from parish ministry. If you report this to a church official and do not want it to be used to end or restrict future ministry, the only possible way of doing so is through a clearly and mutually understood act of confession and absolution. Don't expect that everything you tell your bishop, or denominational supervisor, is under the seal of the confessional; it is not! If you are confident that your misconduct will never be revealed and are absolutely certain that it will never happen again, it may be best for everyone involved that you not reveal it to any ecclesiastical authority. But, you should then remember and seek to follow the eighth and ninth steps of Alcoholics Anonymous:

> 8) We made a list of all the people we had harmed and became willing to make amends to them all.

> 9) We made direct amends whenever possible except when to do so would injure them or others.

Although nothing can erase the injury inflicted by misconduct, "direct amends" might include paying for therapy for someone who has been harmed.

Suggestion 13

If you are currently involved in beyond-the-boundary activity, stop it at once and get the help you need. If you can't stop on your own, surrender to treatment for sexual addiction or whatever has undermined your capacity for self-control. For the sake of yourself and your vocation, as well as your victim or victims, your parish and your marriage and family, this behavior must stop before more harm is done.

Suggestion 14

If uncertain concerning the appropriateness of any present or contemplated behavior, take the following tests:

1) *The test of publicity:* Would you like everyone to know of what you are doing or are tempted to do?

2) *The test of your most respected friends:* Would you like them to know about it? And if they knew, would they approve of it? Would you approve if they were to do it?

3) *The test of projected retrospect:* Is this something you will likely be grateful for ten or twenty years from now, or will you come to regret it?

4) *The test of closest family:* Is this something you would like your wife, children, parents, and brothers and sisters to know about? And if they knew, would they approve of it?

5) *The test of projected consequences:* Will the long-term effect be joy or misery?

If what you are doing or are tempted to do fails even one of these tests, don't do it! Do only that which in the long run is life-affirming and life-fulfilling. Refrain from anything that is ultimately life-denying and life-degrading. You are in ministry to proclaim and share the full and abundant life Christ came to give. Be faithful to that calling!

10

Life-Giving Pastors
Grow in the Grace of God

"We must grow up in every way into him who is the head, into Christ" (Ephesians 4:15).

"Grow in the grace and knowledge of our Lord and Savior Jesus Christ" (2 Peter 3:18).

Of all the diseases that affect children few are more tragic than progeria, a rare affliction that causes children to age more rapidly than they grow, causing them to die of "old age" while still in their childhood. This disorder provides a dramatic illustration of what can happen to us pastors if we age without growing. E. Stanley Jones liked to say, "We don't grow old; we get old when we stop growing." Similarly, Ashley Montagu said:

> The trouble with earthlings is their early adulthood. As long as they are young, they are lovable, open-hearted, tolerant, eager to learn and to collaborate. They can even be induced to play with each other. . . . The ideal should be to prolong childhood up to sixty years. . . . The goal of life is to die young—as late as possible.[1]

Thomas More goes beyond Montagu. He says, "We care for the soul by acknowledging the place of eternal childhood. . . ."[2] So did Jesus: "He called a child whom he put among them, and said, 'Truly, I tell you, unless you change and become like children, you will never enter the kingdom of heaven'" (Matthew 18:2-3). This means that our childhood, and our growing, should be lifelong.

To be effective, life-giving pastors over the long haul, we need to be lifelong learners; that is a professional requirement for long-term ministry. But we are people as well as professionals and that means that we need continued personal growth in grace as well as increased professional competence.

I do not wish to press the distinction between learning and growing too sharply. We certainly grow as we learn and learn as we grow. But it is possible to develop professional competence for ministry without growing spiritually as human beings and as disciples of Christ. A seminary graduate with an outstanding academic record received this evaluation: "He's been an excellent student of theology, but what he has learned seems to have little, if any, personal affect in his life." Such pastors know the right answers but prompt some to say, "They talk the talk but don't walk the walk."

Hearing such comments, we ask, "Is that true of me? Have I been caught up in the professionalism of ministry without corresponding personal growth so that my talk is out of tune with who I am?" It is said that "The theology of some seminary graduates is mostly head knowledge and book learning that is still to be tested in the joys and tragedies of life." This is more of a description than a criticism. Growing takes time.

In the grace of God we are challenged and enabled to grow toward "maturity, to the measure of the full stature of Christ" (Ephesians 4:13). Growing spiritually is a never-ending business. Even heaven may not be a place of static perfection but of eternal growth toward fullness of life. Whatever heaven may be, our present concern is with growing now. What helps growth happen? How do we avoid the tragedy of aging without growing? Once again, I have no pat answers, but I have learned some things in my pilgrimage.

WHAT MIGHT HAVE BEEN?

I sometimes wonder what my life would have been without that early encounter with E. Stanley Jones. While reading his book *The Way*, I was enabled to see that Christianity was not just a way of right belief and right behavior, but instead a way of living by the grace of God. My Lutheran heart was warmed by Jones's Methodist witness, even as John Wesley's heart had been "strangely warmed" by the witness of Martin Luther long before.

In addition to that fresh glimpse of grace, Jones gave me one of the central convictions of my life: I believe that the Christian way is the way we are created to live. That way, said Jones, is written not only in the text of the Bible, but also in the texture of life itself. If this is true, it is an awesome and exceedingly significant fact! Is it true that "all things have been created through Christ and for Christ" and that in Christ "all things hold together" (Colossians 1:16,17)? Are we created to live the life of trust and love that we see in Christ even as a fish is designed for the sea, a bird for the air, our eyes for sight, our ears for sound, a leaf for the sunshine? If that is true, we had best be attentive to Jesus, for in him we see the people we are born to be and the life we are created to live.

The church in which I was brought up confessed that "we are by nature sinful and unclean." I believe what that was trying to say, but not what it may seem to say. Our fallen nature is sinful, but that doesn't mean it's natural for us to sin and unnatural to live as we are created to live. "We have," as Jones liked to say, "been naturalized to the unnatural." We are so acclimated to sinful, self-centered living that we are like alcoholics who need detoxification and who go through painful withdrawal before experiencing joyful sobriety. Living with the self as god is not living as we are designed to live. In Christ, the death of the self as god is the birth of the self as an authentic human being. Then we begin to become the people we are created to be and to live the lives we are designed to live.

My encounter with Jones began years of daily reading of his devotional and other books. Some of my fellow seminary students kidded me for reading "that E. Stanley Jones abundant living stuff," which they equated with the positive thinking of Norman Vincent Peale. From my perspective Jones was far more profound, but I do not wish to disparage Peale. I once heard him preach a powerful New Year's Sunday sermon on the great Pauline benediction, "May the God of hope fill you with all joy and peace in believing that by the power of the Holy Spirit you may abound in hope" (Romans 15:13 RSV), which transformed me from a cynical critic into a thankful worshiper.

From that experience I also realized that we can learn from, and be blessed by, people with whom we disagree. This insight helped me in my study of Luther from whom I have received great blessing while being sickened by some of his comments concerning the Jews. Tolstoy and Ghandi are others for whom I am grateful while at the same time rejecting aspects of Tolstoy's theology and Ghandi's principles and practices concerning food and sex.

Insights That Have Helped Me Grow

"Learn something from everyone you meet" was Jones's repeated recommendation, and I have tried to follow it, not only with people met in person but also those met in books. Among devotional writers, I am especially thankful for Oswald Chambers and began my devotional book, *Authentic Living*, with these quotes from his book *My Utmost for His Highest*:

> To fulfill God's design means entire abandonment to him.
>
> Abandonment to God is of more value than personal holiness.
>
> When we are abandoned to God, he works through us all the time.
>
> In our abandonment we give ourselves to God just as God gives himself to us, without any calculation.
>
> When you get through to abandonment to God, you will be the most surprised and delighted creature on earth; God has you absolutely and has given you your life.
>
> We never know the joy of self-sacrifice until we abandon in every particular. . . . As soon as we abandon, the Holy Ghost gives us an intimation of the joy of Jesus.[3]

This theme of abandonment has become profoundly meaningful to me. Emphasis on sheer grace from God's side and abandonment, surrender, and openness to grace on our side has been central in my understanding of Christian life and thought. Such surrender to any human authority would be self-denigration. The surrender of abandonment and openness to God is self-discovery and self-fulfillment! When we give ourselves to God, God gives us back and lifts us up to "walk in newness of life" (Romans 6:4).

Harry Emerson Fosdick helped me by telling in his autobiography, *The Living of These Days*, of a time when self-reliance was simply ludicrous and of his being sustained by promises and power beyond himself. I think of those things whenever we sing his great hymn, "God of Grace and God of Glory." Luther's emphasis, especially in his *Letters of Spiritual Counsel,* on the fact that the whole way of life for the Christian person consists in just two things, trust in God and love of neighbor, has helped keep me centered on what is central. Because I believe that we are created to be loved and to love, I'd even go beyond Luther to say that the whole way of life for the human person consists, at its center, in trusting the love of God and in relationships of love with one another.

For a time I tried to read everything written by Paul Tournier and was especially blessed by his *Guilt and Grace,* from which I learned that forgiveness does not erase all feelings of guilt but does free us from the condemnation of guilt. If I have really wronged someone, I should feel guilty about it. God's forgiveness does not, and should not, free me of those feelings. But it does give assurance that God still loves and accepts me.

J. N. Kildahl, in *The Holy Spirit and Our Faith,* taught me that God does not help us save ourselves but graciously saves us without our help. He showed me that God does not offer me grace in exchange for my meeting certain conditions and that conditional grace is not grace at all. In *The Cost of Discipleship,* Dietrich Bonhoeffer taught me to beware of cheap grace. What then is left? The costly grace of Christ seen supremely in the cross!

The writings of mystics like Meister Eckhart, books like Brother Lawrence's *Reflections on the Practice of the Presence of God,* together with the witness of the Society of Friends have helped to shape my attitudes toward life in the Divine Presence in whom "we live and move and have our being" (Acts 17:28). At the same time, these Friends and many others from Washington Gladden and Walter Rauschenbusch to Martin Luther King Jr., Robert McAfee Brown, William Sloane Coffin, Tony Campolo, and Walter Wink have forced me to wrestle with the social and political dimensions of the gospel.

The Power of Parents

In a profound sense, Christian spirituality is more *caught* than taught, and when I think of those from whom I caught it, I think first of my mother. She was born in Norway, but had little of the stereotypical

143

Scandinavian reserve. She sang songs of trust and joy in our farmhouse kitchen and witnessed in a simple, natural way to living in daily companionship with one of whom she often said, "Jesus is my friend, I on him depend." Her childlike trust, warmth, and outgoing compassion for people were powerful influences in my formative years.

Dad was born in a log cabin on the Minnesota frontier and had an abundance of Nordic reserve combined with commitment to integrity and fairness. He also had a temper. Once, while still in grade school, I did something Dad thought foolish while trying to help him put up a fence. He lost his temper and shouted in anger, "Don't be so damned stupid!" Several hours later he turned to me and said, "I want to ask you to forgive me for talking to you that way. You are not stupid and I should not have used that kind of language. Please forgive me." As I reflect on that memory, it strikes me as an example of what it is to be a Christian example. Christian example doesn't say, "I'm perfect; imitate me." It says, "I, too, am sinful; please forgive me."

Another attitude caught from both parents was a sense of awe before the mystery of creation. As children, my twin brother and I walked beyond the farmyard grove to marvel at the splendor of the starry night and listened to Dad telling of distances measured in light years and Mother speaking prayerfully of the greatness of a God who could create such wonders.

Starry skies are still awesome to me. I think of how light takes 100,000 years to travel from one edge of our Milky Way to the other and of how starlight that was seen by Abraham and by the astrologers seeking Jesus has barely begun its journey across our galaxy, which is only one of billions of galaxies in our incomprehensively vast universe. How did all this come to be? Doesn't everything have to come from something? But where then did the original something come from? It seems impossible! There should be neither God, nor universe, nor life, nor me! Yet here I am, marvelling at the wonder of it all!

As I ponder such mystery, I think Mulford Q. Sibley was right when he said, "Nobody knows enough to be an atheist." We can be agnostic and say, "I simply don't know." But before the awesome physical universe and the even greater wonder of life within it, how dare we say, "There is no God!"

teaching, the Bible is a means of grace that invites, evokes, and enables lives of faith, hope, and love. Therefore, I read and reread the Bible, seeking light and assurance of love for my venture of living.

Encounter with Whiston

The specific pattern of my daily devotional life was significantly shaped by an encounter with Charles Whiston, an Episcopal priest whose central mission in life, when I met him twenty-five years ago, was to deepen the spiritual life of seminary faculties. He visited Luther Seminary, and several of us met with him and attended several of his retreats. Under his influence, a small group met regularly in one of the small dormitory chapels to do our daily devotions silently in each other's presence and for personal sharing and prayer. Another faculty member and I covenanted to be "soul brothers" for mutual encouragement and mentoring. During our meetings we checked up on each other, shared our joys and frustrations, and prayed together.

Over the years, I have continued to follow some of the habits I caught from Whiston. He later wrote a book on prayer, but the quotations I share with you come from mimeographed sheets he handed out to us and from notes taken during our retreats together.

Whiston suggested that our waking thoughts be of promises of God, such as, "Do not fear, for I have redeemed you; I have called you by name and you are mine" (Isaiah 43:1). He urged us to begin each day with a prayer of "pre-acceptance" of God's blessing, such as the following:

> Thank you, gracious Father, for every good gift this day will bring. Thank you for grace sufficient for every moment. Thank you that nothing in life nor death, this day, can separate me from you and your love in Christ Jesus. [4]

We were encouraged to listen with the ears of faith and to hear Christ saying, "I have chosen you and I love you. I have given my life for you. Therefore, you do not belong to yourself; you belong to me. In trust of my love, give me yourself for today." Then in response came prayer of surrender:

Such thoughts may drive some to doubt and despair but they give me a great sense of exhilaration and gratitude for the privilege of a brief visit to this little planet to experience this strange thing called life, and to hear promises evoking trust that the heart of the universe beats with Christ-like love.

Teachers Who Moved as Well as Taught Me

In addition to my parents, many professors and teachers influenced me by their warmth as well as their wisdom. George Aus talked about "the living God actively engaged in history with a redemptive purpose," with a sense of knowing the one of whom he spoke. When Alvin Rogness referred to "resting back in the arms of God," it was as a child cradled in love.

When Gerhard Frost told of having lived half his life as a coper and of then coming a time when he could no longer cope, but could only live by the grace of God, he spoke to my experience and to my need. Frost also taught me that some of God's best gifts are not on the top shelves to be reached by climbing up but rather on the bottom shelves to be received by kneeling down. Poets like Frost encouraged me to see all of life as an adventure in spiritual growth. When I went to hear him speak on "The Pastor's Devotional Life," I expected a presentation on daily disciplines, but what I heard were reflections on Robert Frost's "The Death of a Hired Man." I was surprised but not disappointed, and I learned that day that nurture for spiritual growth comes from secular as well as religious sources.

Nurture from Scripture

As shared earlier, it has been my habit for many years to spend the first half-hour of most days reading the Bible in an annotated edition. Reading for a specified amount of time, instead of a certain number chapters, frees me to take my time, in checking footnotes and cross references. My goal is not to read straight through the Bible once a year (it takes me longer than that), but instead to understand it better and above all, to let God speak to me.

Apart from the Bible, we would not know Jesus. Apart from Jesus we really do not know the Bible. With Jesus as Lord of every text

Gracious, Lord Jesus Christ: in response to your love for me, I surrender myself anew this day to you. I yield to you all that I am and all that I have, to be wholly and unconditionally yours for your using. Take me away from my preoccupation with myself and enable me to live with self-forgetful trust and self-giving love. Use me this day as you will, where you will, with whom you will. In your name I pray. Amen.

Lest there be misunderstanding, I stress again that such surrender is not self-denigration leading to slavery but self-discovery leading to freedom. Yielding to Christ is yielding to "life in fullness" (John 10:10 NEB). When we sincerely pray, "Your will be done" (Matthew 6:10) our pretending-to-be-God self dies and our true human self is born.

Prayer of surrender was followed prayer of preparation for Bible reading:

O Lord Jesus Christ, in response to your love and invitation I come to sit at your feet, to look up at you, to listen to you, that I may again meet you, surrender to you, and serve and obey you. Meet me now, speak to me, give yourself to me to make me yours for your using. Amen.

Then came a time of quiet devotional pondering of Scripture followed by a period of intercessory prayer. When Whiston told us that he prayed for 6,000 people every day, we asked, "How in the world do you do that?" Whiston replied that he saw himself on the screen of his imagination being welcomed and embraced by the love of Christ. He then visualized this cosmic Christ turning him around, standing behind him with hands on his shoulders, and saying, "Now look with me at the people I love. Receive from me the gift of my caring and compassion for each of them." With that set of mind and heart, Whiston would then go through his list of 6,000 names, lifting up each one in the caring context of the compassion of Christ. Thoughts of special need would prompt some specific prayer petitions, such as, "Heal and strengthen Mary," but most of the intercessions were without petitions. No words were necessary. Thinking of each person with the compassion of Christ was sufficient. He began each time of intercession with a prayer such as:

O Lord Jesus Christ, I now look with you at these persons. Give me the gift of your caring and compassion for them as I now pray with you for each of them.

Whiston's habit was to spend about two hours a day, five days a week, in daily intercession for those 6,000 people. Remembering that Jesus taught us not only to pray the Lord's Prayer in the words of the New Testament text but to "pray, then like this" (Matthew 6:9 RSV), Whiston also prayed the Lord's Prayer in intercessory forms, such as:

Our Father in heaven,
May Bill and Mary live today with reverence toward you.
Reign and rule in their lives.
Do your will in each of them as it is done in heaven.
Give them the things they need for today.
Forgive them their sins as they forgive those who sin against them.
Bring them through their of trials and temptations and deliver
    them from every evil.
For the kingdom, the power, and the glory are yours forever.
Amen.

I have never attempted to match the extent, pace, or duration of Whiston's intercessions. Even though 6,000 is way beyond me, I can manage about sixty, beginning with family, coworkers, persons known to be in special need, and several pages of clergy, associates-in-ministry, and lay leaders in our synod handbook.

Although I do not believe that prayers are magical incantations, the practice of intercession is meaningful for me. In Christ we are co-carers, and even co-creators, with God. Like other loving actions, prayerful caring for one another is of significance. We can't measure the difference intercession makes, but we need not be excessively concerned about that. At the very least, I know that it certainly affects my attitudes and actions toward those for whom I pray. Beyond that, I entrust these prayers, along with these people, to the love of God, who hears every prayer.

In accord with my, perhaps unusual, circadian rhythms I am usually wide awake by 5 A.M., and that's when I get up and have my quiet time which includes Bible and devotional reading, journaling, and prayer. I scan the headlines in the morning paper but don't read the paper until later while riding my exercise bicycle. Thoughts concerning next Sunday's sermon or something else I must do often come to mind, but I try hard to resist the temptation to use this devotional time as preparation time and am usually, but not always, successful. By about 6:30 I begin to feel sleepy and, so that I won't awaken my wife, retire to a cot in the basement for my first nap of the day. By 7:15 or so, I am again awake and we have breakfast together.

Each of us has our own rhythms and must discover the best time of day for devotional reflection. One time is not necessarily better than another. Paul Tournier wrote of how he liked to have his devotional time early in the morning, but his wife preferred hers later in the day. This helped me understand that Carol and I were respecting our individuality and not being unfaithful to each other when we chose different times and forms of devotional life. Kahlil Gibran may have had this in mind when he said in *The Prophet*, "Let there be spaces in your togetherness." We should not seek to impose our pattern on anyone. One member of our Whiston-sharing group did intercessions during his daily walk. Others may do them in the car. Instead of fuming at stop lights and in snarled traffic, we can use these times of enforced waiting for intercession. Precisely when we do it doesn't much matter, but the fact that we do it matters a great deal.

More recently, my devotional quiet time has included writing as well as reading and praying. Years ago, after reading John A. Sanford's *Dreams: God's Forgotten Language*, I kept a dream diary for a time and found it to be interesting and insightful, but until recently have not been disciplined in keeping a daily journal. I was envious of some who spoke of its meaning but was always deterred by the thought that it was laborious and time consuming. As mentioned earlier, Ronald Klug's book *How to Keep a Spiritual Journal* liberated me from such a legalistic understanding. I now see journaling as a gift to be received and not as a duty to be fulfilled. Since reading his book I have been jotting details of the day, together with thoughts and reflections, in a spiral-bound notebook. It takes only a few minutes each day, and I find it meaningful and it is a practice I intend to continue.

Help from Others

Except for the time when I covenanted with a "soul brother," I've never had a spiritual director. But am impressed by the testimony of those who have found this to be helpful and recommend it to you. I have been blessed by personal association with people such as Gerhard Frost and Herman Preus who were visitation pastors with me and, although never officially designated as such, significant spiritual mentors.

As already mentioned, small group experiences for personal sharing and prayer have been meaningful. We often encourage our members to be involved in small groups and should set an example by doing so ourselves. For us, the most personal sharing can occur if the group is composed of fellow clergy and spouses, and other like-minded people from congregations other than our own. In this regard, I recommend George S. Johnson's book *Starting Small Groups and Keeping Them Going* [5] and Richard C. Meyer's *One Anothering: Biblical Building Blocks for Small Groups.* This creative book "takes off" from the many biblical sayings, such as to "love one another," "pray for one another," and "bear one another's' burden." [6]

Devotional sharing with our synod staff was also a blessing. We took turns leading the opening devotions at our weekly staff meetings and had a time of intercession for congregations and pastors as well as for those known to be in situations of special need. We informed the congregations ahead of time that we would be praying for them, asked them to share specific prayer requests, and invited them to pray for us. One of our congregations follows a similar practice and prays for a portion of the membership during each staff meeting. Members are called in advance and told they will be remembered in this way and asked for their prayer requests. I am told that both the staff and the membership find this practice meaningful and am sure it deepens their bonding with one another.

Self-Talk

By accident or providence, I recently read a little book entitled *What to Say When You Talk to Yourself* by Shad Helmstetter and learned for the first time of the "self-talk" movement. [7] Even though I think there is a lot of fluff in this emphasis, I also believe these people may be on

150

to something that can be significant for our spiritual growth. Living by the grace of God should have something to say about how we talk to ourselves. It certainly did for the apostle Paul, who gave an example of how we Christians should talk to ourselves when he said, "I can do all things through Christ who strengthens me" (Philippians 4:13). After receiving the promise "My grace is sufficient for you, for my power is made perfect in weakness" (2 Corinthians 12:9), it is likely he often told himself, "God's grace is sufficient for me," and "My strength is not in myself but in the gracious power of God." Until reading Helmstetter, I'd given little thought to how I talk to myself, but with his encouragement, and with the apostle Paul as a model, I am now trying to talk to myself in ways that are appropriate for a person claimed by Christ.

People in Twelve Step groups often warn against "stinkin' thinkin.'" So did the apostle Paul when he says, "Let the same mind be in you that was in Christ Jesus" (Philippians 2:5) and again, "Whatever is true, whatever is honorable, whatever is just, whatever is pure, whatever is pleasing, whatever is commendable, if there is any excellence and if there is anything worthy of praise, think about these things" (Philippians 4:8). Because less censorship is involved, what we say to ourselves is more revealing of who we are than what we say to others. When our self-talk reveals stinkin' thinkin', we are in need of repentance which literally means a change of mind. Thanks to the gracious presence of the Holy Spirit at work in both our conscious and unconscious minds, there is healing for stinkin' thinkin' and hope that we might increasingly have the mind of Christ.

Worship: Burden or Blessing?

Except for being in a different congregation almost every Sunday, my experience of worship as a bishop was similar to that of a parish pastor. I was usually up front preaching and leading. But now there are Sundays without such responsibilities, and I am free from having to think about what comes next or what to say in the sermon. As a worshiper, even more than as presider and preacher, I am often struck by what a great privilege it is to be part of a community centered in Jesus Christ. We are blessed to be able to sing and pray together, to hear the witness of Scripture read and then proclaimed in a meaningful sermon. Even if the music and sermon are mediocre, just being there with others in this Christ-centered community is an uplifting and life-enriching experience.

This is not to suggest that worship as blessing is totally missing when I am in the chancel, but I must confess that there are times when preaching and presiding feels more like a burden than a blessing. For the pastor, the responsibilities of leading worship can be more exhausting than exhilarating.

What can make worship a blessing for the pastor as well as the parishioners? One important factor relates to how we see ourselves and what we are doing. If we see ourselves as performers, putting on a show for the people, it is no wonder that preaching and leading worship wears us out. Few of us are sufficiently creative to come up with great shows that will wow the audience and evoke weekly accolades of affirmation and appreciation that are the equivalent of enthusiastic applause. When our performance fails to create such a positive response, our valiant effort may leave us feeling rejected and depressed, as well as exhausted.

But when we see ourselves as participants with our parishioners, worshiping together in a grace-centered community, and preach to ourselves as well as to them, we too can be blessed. I once heard George Aus say, "I never preach to others without also preaching to myself." As pastors we have leadership roles that make our experience of worship different from that of our parishioners, but it is not entirely different. We stand together under the mercy and judgment of God. We break bread together and, as the old saying puts it, "We are like one beggar telling other beggars where we can all find food."

In our continued sinfulness we will never be totally free of the self-preoccupation that makes us anxious to please and keeps us wondering what others think of us. But, at the same time, we can be mindful of the fact that we are "servants of Christ and stewards of the mysteries of God" (1 Corinthians 4:1).

I read of a British preacher who was told by a panicked usher that the King of England and his entourage had just entered the church. The preacher's first response was shock in fearful recognition that "I will preside and preach in the presence of the King of England!" But then he said to himself (in words of significant self-talk), "Why does the presence of the King of England so frighten me? I preside and preach every Sunday in the presence of the King of Kings!"

Those of us who preach regularly are deprived of the privilege of hearing the preaching of others. To make up for this loss, I often hear several early morning radio sermons, including the *Protestant Hour*, the *Lutheran Hour*, and the rebroadcast of last week's worship from Central Lutheran Church in Minneapolis, and end the day with *Lutheran Vespers* and Billy Graham. When too preoccupied with last-minute review of my own sermon to listen to others, I often tape them to hear later. When a meaningful sermon speaks to me, it not only nourishes me personally but also renews my faith in the life-giving possibilities of preaching. When a sermon doesn't minister to me, it still reminds me that people come to worship hungry and thirsty for life-giving nourishment and that I should seek to preach as one serving them a meal and not as one lecturing about food. Just before preaching, I often find myself praying Harry Emerson Fosdick's pre-sermon prayer: "Dear Lord, I believe that someone here needs this message. Help me to reach that person."

Self-Care for the Care of Others

Focussing on personal spiritual growth may seem selfish and self-centered, but it need not be. I am often struck by the instruction of the flight attendant: "If you are traveling with a child or someone who needs your care, put on your oxygen mask before assisting that person." This reminds us that we who care for others must sometimes first care for ourselves. We who are called to give must first receive. Such receiving is an act of sanctified selfishness. For the Christian pastor, lifelong growing as a child of God abounds in personal blessing, but it also provides strength for the fulfillment of long-term, life-giving ministry.

Self-care also involves time for recreation and just plain fun. As noted earlier, Ashley Montagu said that one characteristic of children is that "they can even be induced to play with each other." Growing in grace involves playful as well as serious times, times of laughter as well as times of tears. When abandoned to the grace of God, we are free to live and love with abandonment, enjoying in fullness all of the good things and good times God provides for us. I sometimes wonder if on Judgment Day we will be called to account for all of the proper pleasures we have failed to enjoy! Growing in grace enables us to face and feel the joyful, as well as tragic, dimensions of life.

Learnings Shared for Your Encouragement

In summary, I again share some things that I have learned. They are important to me and I hope they are also significant for you.

1. Personal spiritual growth and professional pastoral competence are both essential for life-giving pastoral ministry. Personal spiritual growth without professional competence results in warm but shallow ministry. Professional competence without personal spiritual growth results in cold and formal ministry in which the pastor as person becomes increasingly absent. Effective ministry requires both growing and learning, both compassion and competence.

2. Just as competence requires lifelong learning, spiritual formation requires lifelong growing. Learning and growing are life-time adventures. There is always more to learn and growing "to maturity, to the measure of the full stature of Christ" (Ephesians 4:13) is a never-ending project.

3. As learning requires time for serious study, growing in grace requires time for solitude, quiet reflection, and prayer. We can buy a degree from a diploma mill, but we can't purchase an education or buy pastoral competence. To become educated and competent takes lots of time and lots of hard work. So also, a dramatic conversion or powerful experience of being struck by grace can transform our lives, but these do not instantly convey spiritual maturity. The apostle Paul didn't start preaching the day after his encounter with Christ on the Damascus Road. He "went away into Arabia" (Galatians 1:17), to think things over and make sense of what had happened. Thanks to slow travel and times in jail, he had much opportunity for continued reflection. We who aren't "blessed" with enforced solitude need to make time for it ourselves. That is most likely to happen when we realize that reflective, prayerful solitude is a treasure to be received and not a trial to be endured. Like times of worship, it can be a blessing and not a burden, a gift and not a chore. As lovers cherish their trysting times, we too can come to look forward to trysting time with God.

Although it is true that "prayer is the soul's sincere desire unuttered or expressed," and that in attitude we can "pray constantly" (1 Thessalonians 5:17), it is unlikely that this will be our continual desire and attitude for very long unless reinforced by specific times of conscious and deliberate meditation and prayer. Attitudes and habits of the heart are shaped and sustained by daily disciplines of thought and action.

4. An abundance of growth-giving blessings are available to nurture and strengthen us. Among these are the Bible, great classics of devotional literature, writings by contemporary authors that speak to our condition, guidance concerning devotion and intercession such as that shared from Charles Whiston, small groups for personal sharing and prayer, our own discipline in journaling, the blessing of worshiping together, and being strengthened by a prayer partner, mentor or spiritual director. Nourishing treasures are available for us. All that is needed is that we take time to receive them.

5. Every day is a new beginning and a new opportunity. We especially need to remember this fact on days when we fail to keep our quiet time of trysting with God. You may decide to be more disciplined in your Bible and devotional reading and to follow the Whiston pattern of intercession. Things will go well for a while, but then there will be a string of early morning meetings or emergencies that cause you to skip your quiet time and you will be tempted to give up on it altogether. But the only real failure is to forget that each day is a day for starting over again. Resolving to set aside an hour a day, seven days a week, is probably too much for most of us. How about one-half hour a day for five days? Or fifteen minutes a day, three to four days week? Or five minutes, two to three days a week? Even one minute a day is infinitely more than nothing! Willpower and determination are often required to begin the discipline of a daily quiet time, but the key, once again, is not in self-centered struggle but in self-giving surrender. Taking time for quiet, careful reflection becomes a joyful habit when we discover that it is not an obligation we have to carry but a source of strength that lifts and carries us.

6. It is futile and counter-productive to be preoccupied with measuring our spiritual growth. When we are measuring, we get in the way of our growing. William Temple said, "Humility is not thinking less of ourselves than of other people. It is not thinking of ourselves one way or the other at all!" So too with spiritual growth—it is growth in self-forgetfulness, not self-preoccupation.

Alvin Rogness told of a pastor 100 years ago who learned that a parishioner was dying on the other side of the lake in the mountain community he served. Although it was late and a storm was brewing, he got into his boat, rowed across the lake, and was with the dying parishioner and his family through the night. Then, as dawn was breaking, he rowed back home across the stormy lake. As he rowed, he thought to himself, "The word will get out. People will talk of what a courageous and caring pastor I am. I will be praised for my bravery and compassion." Then came another thought, "What a terrible self-centered sinner I am to think of myself and of what people will think of me." This was followed by yet another thought, "To be so aware of my sinfulness is certainly a sign of my spiritual maturity."

This story witnesses to the endless cycle of sinful self-preoccupation in each of us. We are, as Luther often said, "curved in upon ourselves." Facing this reality, we cry with the apostle Paul, "Miserable creature that I am, who is there to rescue me out of this body doomed to death? God alone, through Jesus Christ our Lord! Thanks be to God!" (Romans 7:24-25 NEB).

In such times, we learn again that we live by the grace of God and that the gift of self-forgetful humility is not achieved by our striving but is received in those moments when give ourselves with abandonment to the love of God and in loving service of others. Then we are children again, yearning for more of life, open to learn and to grow, willing and working to be life-giving in all that we say and do.

Notes

Introduction

1. Doan, Gilbert E., Jr. *The Preaching of F. W. Robertson*. Philadelphia: Fortress Press, 1964, p. 196.

2. Ginott, Haim. Quoted by Ann Landers. Minneapolis *Star Tribune*. March 23, 1996, p. E2.

1. Life-Giving Pastors Live by the Grace of God

1. Jones, E. Stanley. *The Way*. Nashville: Abingdon Press, 1946.

2. Erdahl, Lowell O., *Authentic Living*. Nashville: Abingdon Press, 1979.

3. Tillich, Paul. *The Shaking of the Foundations*. New York: Charles Scribner's Sons, 1948, pp. 161-162.

4. Niebuhr, Reinhold. *The Nature and Destiny of Man*, chapter IV, "Wisdom, Grace and Power." See especially "The Biblical Doctrine of Grace" and "Grace as Power in, and as Mercy Towards, Man," New York: Charles Scribner's Sons, 1959, pp. 98-126.

5. Tournier, Paul. *The Strong and the Weak*. Philadelphia: Westminster Press, 1963, pp. 20-21.

6. Gray, Thomas. "Elegy Written in a Country Churchyard." *College Survey of English Literature*. New York: Harcourt, Brace & Co., 1951, p. 577.

2. Life-Giving Pastors Bond with Their People

1. Erdahl, Lowell O., and Carol Erdahl. *Be Good to Each Other: An Open Letter on Marriage*. Minneapolis: Augsburg, 1991, p. 25.

2. Housman, A. E. *A Shropshire Lad*. From poem XLI, "In my own shire if I was sad." London: Harrap, 1984, pp. 61-62.

3. Friedman, Edward H. *Generation to Generation: Family Process in Church and Synagogue*. New York: Guilford Press, 1985, p. 271.

4. Edwards, Mark U., Jr. *Printing, Propaganda, and Martin Luther*. Berkeley, Los Angeles: University of California Press, 1994, pp. 11, 170.

5. Stevenson, J. W. *God in My Unbelief*. New York: Harper and Row, 1963, pp. 53-54.

3. Life-Giving Pastors Exercise Gift-Evoking Leadership

1. Bennis, Warren. *On Becoming a Leader*. Reading, Mass.: Addison-Wesley, 1994, p. 1.

2. Heifetz, Ronald. *Leadership Without Easy Answers.* Cambridge, Mass.: Belknap Press, 1994, pp. 14-15.

3. Ibid, p. 187.

4. Ibid, pp. 148-149.

5. De Pree, Max. *Leadership Is an Art.* New York: Doubleday, 1989, p. 11.

6. Covey, Stephen R. *The Seven Habits of Highly Effective People.* New York: Simon & Schuster, 1989, p. 277.

7. Heifetz, p. 326.

4. *Life-Giving Pastors Are Lifelong Learners*

1. Durant, Will. Quoted in *Words of Wisdom,* by William Safire and Leonard Safir. Beleuvue, Wash.: S & S, 1990, p. 239.

2. Bennis, p. XIV.

3. Scherer, Paul. Quoted by Elizabeth Achtemeier. Chapter entitled "The Canon as the Voice of the Living God," in *Reclaiming the Bible for the Church,* Carl E. Braaten and Robert W. Jenson, eds. Grand Rapids, Mich.: Erdmann's Publishing Company, 1995, p. 122.

4. Bennis, p. 48.

5. Klug, Ronald. *How to Keep a Spiritual Journal: A Guide to Journal Keeping for Inner Growth and Personal Discovery.* Minneapolis: Augsburg, 1993.

5. *Life-Giving Pastors Have Something to Say and Say It Well*

1. Walther, C. F. W. *God's No and God's Yes: Proper Distinction Between Law and Gospel* (condensed by Walter C. Pieper). St. Louis: Concordia, 1973, Thesis XIII, pp. 9, 67.

2. McCroskey, James C. *An Introduction to Rhetorical Communication.* Englewood Clifffs, N.J.: Prentice Hall, 1968, p. 213.

3. Flowers, Linda. *Good Advice on Writing.* Edited by William Safire and Leonard Safir. New York: Simon & Schuster, 1992, p. 36.

4. Ibid., p. 102.

5. Reuter, Alvin. *Making Good Preaching Better.* Collegeville, Minn.: Liturgical Press, 1997.

6. For additional suggestions and a more detailed exposition of my perspectives on preaching, see *Preaching for the People,* Nashville: Abingdon, 1976; and *Better Preaching: Evaluating the Sermon,* St. Louis: Concordia, 1977.